prettylittle presents

pretty little
presents

LARK

SENIOR EDITOR
Valerie Van Arsdale Shrader

EDITOR
Larry Shea

ART DIRECTOR
Megan Kirby

ART PRODUCTION
Jeff Hamilton

ASSISTANT EDITOR
Mark Bloom

ILLUSTRATIONS
Susan McBride

TEMPLATES
Orrin Lundgren

PHOTOGRAPHER
Stewart O'Shields

COVER DESIGNER
Carol Morse Barnao

LARK
An Imprint of Sterling Publishing
387 Park Avenue South
New York, NY 10016

First Paperback Edition 2013
© 2009, Lark Books, A Division of Sterling Publishing Co., Inc.

ISBN 13: 978-1-60059-401-4 (hardcover) 978-1-4547-0855-1 (paperback)

The Library of Congress has cataloged the hardcover edition as follows:
Pretty little presents / editor, Valerie Van Arsdale Shrader.
    p. cm.
Includes index.
ISBN 978-1-60059-401-4 (hc-plc with jacket : alk. paper)
1. Handicraft. I. Shrader, Valerie Van Arsdale.
TT157.P7445 2009
745.5--dc22

2008052581

Distributed in Canada by Sterling Publishing
c/o Canadian Manda Group, 165 Dufferin Street
Toronto, Ontario, Canada M6K 3H6
Distributed in the United Kingdom by GMC Distribution Services
Castle Place, 166 High Street, Lewes, East Sussex, England BN7 1XU
Distributed in Australia by Capricorn Link (Australia) Pty. Ltd.
P.O. Box 704, Windsor, NSW 2756, Australia

For information about custom editions, special sales, and premium and corporate purchases, please contact Sterling Special Sales at 800-805-5489 or specialsales@sterlingpublishing.com.

Email academic@larkbooks.com for information about desk and examination copies. The complete policy can be found at larkcrafts.com.

Manufactured in China

2 4 6 8 10 9 7 5 3 1

larkcrafts.com

contents

introduction

When it's time to give a present, we all hope our choice will be met with a response like "How thoughtful!" or "It's just what I always wanted!" If a gift instead evokes, "It's the thought that counts," it usually means you've disappointed rather than delighted. Wouldn't you prefer that your gift causes a genuine smile, and not a forced grin?

When you give one of the presents in this book, that old expression takes on a whole new meaning. Now what counts is that you thought enough of someone to give a gift that's handmade, one-of-a-kind, and just plain beautiful. Something that holds within it a little of your time, talent, and creativity. When you show up at a shower with a gift you've crafted yourself, like the Nesting Instinct tote bag on page 116, the delighted mom-to-be will know just how much you care about her and her baby. The only problem: You'll have raised the bar for every future gift-giving occasion to new heights, as everyone wonders what you'll bring next. Not to worry—that's why you'll find another 28 fabulous projects to choose from in these pages.

No matter what the occasion or how picky the potential recipient, *Pretty Little Presents* has a gift you'll be able to make and want to give. The projects are arranged to provide plenty of "wow-worthy" presents for hosts, new homeowners, newlyweds, birthday celebrants, and expectant parents. Going to a dinner party? Take along a wrapped bottle of wine (In the Bag, page 40) for the hosts or the All Buttoned Up napkin rings (page 42) for the table. Have a friend who's always traveling to exotic spots (or just dreaming of them)? She's sure to love the Take Note notebook cover (page 32) or the Passport, Please document holder (page 66). Got a bridal or baby shower coming up? The chorus of "aws" will be deafening when everyone sees you've made Hearts on a String (page 92) or Hello, Doll Faces (page 124).

After making and giving away a few projects, you'll probably want to keep some of these beautiful objects for yourself. Luckily, there's another old saying that applies here: "Charity begins at home." Don't you and your home deserve—in fact, *need*—some pretty little presents of your own? Don't bother to wait for a special occasion. You'll appreciate an unexpected "just because" present from yourself even more. After all, it's the thought that counts.

presents basics

Unwrapping the secret to perfect gift giving for any occasion is easy—simply sew it yourself! This chapter provides you with the information you need about tools, materials, and techniques to make all the pretty little presents in this book. Refer to it often while you work, and you'll never go empty-handed again.

*presents*tools

Unless you're new to sewing, a quick gathering expedition around your craft space should yield the tools you need. Use the **Basic Presents Tool Kit,** below, as your guide. Make sure you have everything on hand before you begin. Nothing is worse than stopping to search for straight pins once the creative juices have started to flow.

Basic Presents Tool Kit

- *Sharp sewing scissors (for fabric)*
- *Craft scissors (for paper)*
- *Rotary cutter and mat*
- *Pinking shears*
- *Sewing machine*
- *Sewing machine needles*
- *Hand-sewing needles*
- *Measuring tape*
- *Transparent ruler*
- *Tailor's chalk or water-soluble fabric marker*
- *Needle threader*
- *Seam ripper*
- *Iron*
- *Straight pins*
- *Thread*
- *Scrap paper (for patterns)*
- *Pencil with an eraser*

SEWING SCISSORS

Be sharp! Save these scissors for fabric only. Using them to cut paper will dull the blades, making them useless on fabric. If you're shopping for a new pair, quality is worth the extra cost. Give the scissors a test run at the store before purchasing them. If they fit comfortably in your grip as you snip, you'll be assured a lifetime of happy cutting.

A welcome addition to any sewing basket is a good pair of fine-tipped scissors, such as embroidery scissors. They quickly slip into smaller spaces, making them easy to maneuver when clipping tight curves or when doing tiny detail work.

CRAFT SCISSORS

Reach for these scissors when cutting anything *but* fabric. An all-purpose pair should be of moderate length for ease of use when cutting out curves and corners on paper patterns and templates. Don't break the bank when purchasing these scissors. In fact, you might already have more pairs lurking about than you dare admit.

PINKING SHEARS

The zigzag pattern made by these shears prevents fabric from fraying. Use them to trim a seam or add a decorative touch to any edge.

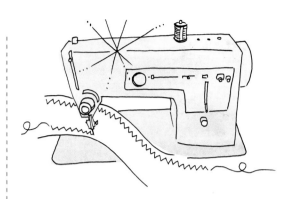

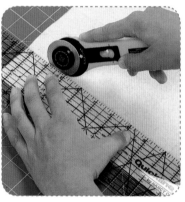

ROTARY CUTTER AND MAT

Quilters popularized rotary cutters because their sharp rolling wheels quickly slice through multiple layers of fabric. Now many crafters use them for many of their fabric-cutting needs. You'll find that some projects substitute this tool for scissors. If you choose to use a rotary cutter, always use it with a self-healing mat. Aside from saving your work surface, the mat has a printed grid that provides an extra measure of accuracy when you cut.

SEWING MACHINE

All of these projects require a sewing machine. Even if you're an experienced seamstress, a quick review of the most basic rules for machine stitching can help you as you work. When sewing thicker fabrics, make sure to reduce the pressure on the foot and use a longer stitch. This simple step allows the fabric to glide through the feeder. For any seam that needs a good anchor, backstitch at the beginning and end of the seam to secure the stitching. Use the zigzag stitch on raw edges to prevent the fabric from fraying. Change the presser foot as needed for the task at hand whenever you are straight stitching, zigzagging, or applying a zipper.

NEEDLE KNOW-HOW

Don't fall for one size fits all when it comes to machine needles. All-purpose needles are fine if you sew only one type of fabric. Use sharp needles when sewing silks or woven fabrics, but make sure to change to ballpoint needles for knits. The smooth ball-shaped point slips between the knit fibers rather than piercing them.

SEWING MACHINE NEEDLES

Grrr! Broken needle! Dull needle! Need we say more? Except that the *real* frustration comes when you find you don't have extras on hand. Machine needles are inexpensive, and it pays to purchase several packs at a time. Give yourself a gift by getting in the habit of starting each project with a new needle; it has to be one of life's most economical luxuries. Indulge.

HAND-SEWING NEEDLES

A variety-pack of needles is all you need to handle the general sewing in the projects of this book. The range of needle sizes allows you to sew together most common fabrics. Some projects call for an embroidery needle, which has a longer eye to accommodate thicker embroidery floss.

NEEDLE THREADER

You think you have it, only to find you've missed the mark. Then you try again. Attempting to thread a needle over and over doesn't do much for your self-esteem. Save yourself the trouble by using a needle threader. Simply push the thin wire loop of this tiny tool through the eye of the needle, insert the thread, and pull the loop out.

SEAM RIPPER

A seam ripper is probably the most satisfying of all sewing supplies to own because it can undo mistakes in no time. Like the perfect gift, it keeps on giving by continually providing you with a second chance at perfection.

MEASURING TAPE AND TRANSPARENT RULER

Somehow it just doesn't feel like you're sewing unless you have a tape measure curled on the cutting table or draped around your neck, ready to measure on command. But a transparent ruler can't be beat for drawing a straight line or marking small measurements—a must-have when making these pretty *little* presents. You can also use the ruler as a straight edge when you're using a rotary cutter.

FABRIC MARKING PENS AND TAILOR'S CHALK

Now you see it, now you don't. These marking tools aren't magic, but their lines do vanish once their job is done. Use a water-soluble fabric marker when marking sewing or cutting lines and embroidery designs. The ink will disappear with plain water. It's always best to test a marker on a fabric scrap since the dyes in some fabrics can make the ink hard to remove. Tailor's chalk leaves dust on the surface of the fibers, but you'll find it easy to brush the marks away once they've served their purpose—no trick about it.

PINS

Traditional, short metal pins with small heads will do the job, but they're no fun. The longer pins with plastic or glass heads are easier to handle and can make pinning a more colorful experience.

IRON

Hot, hot, hot! The secret's out. Irons aren't just for getting rid of wrinkles. This invaluable tool also sets seams and hems, and it applies the heat to fusible web, transfers, and appliqués.

CHOP CHOP

After sewing and trimming a corner, it's time to turn the fabric right side out. Wait a minute! The corner still looks all bunched up. What to do? Grab a chopstick or a knitting needle! Use it to push the corner out before pressing, and you'll be done in no time, with perfect results.

ASSORTED TOOLS

As you scan the "What You Need" section for each project, you might see other tools listed. These can include:

CRAFT KNIFE

The razor-sharp, changeable blades will cut through paper, cardboard, and vinyl.

GLUE AND ADHESIVES

Use these in lieu of stitching to affix a button or add an embellishment. Adhesives also come in handy when you want to baste quickly without stitches.

STAPLE GUN AND STAPLES

Use the staples to attach fabric to a frame.

SETTING TOOLS

Some snaps, eyelets, and decorative studs require the use of a special tool to attach them to the fabric. You can find these tools wherever you purchase your notions. Follow the manufacturer's instructions.

EMBROIDERY HOOP

Two simple wooden circles, one inside the other, hold fabric taut when you need to embroider.

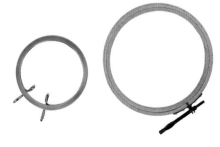

presents materials

If you've been sewing for a while, you probably have a rather large stash of fabrics, notions, and lovely embellishments on hand. Of course you *can* use what you already have, *or* you can use these projects as an excuse to go see what's new at your favorite fabric or craft store (as if you needed an excuse).

THREADS

You can't go wrong choosing a quality polyester thread for all-purpose machine and hand sewing. This versatile thread sews strong seams, essential for projects designed to hold other items, such as the Passport, Please wallet (page 66) and the In the Bag wine cozy (page 40).

FLOSSES

Some projects incorporate a touch of embroidery as an embellishment. Use multi-strand embroidery floss in cotton, silk, or rayon to add these decorative highlights.

INTERFACING

Interfacing adds support and structure to your sewn presents. It comes in different weights, but most projects use light- or medium-weight interfacing for subtle shaping. For projects that need to retain their shape, such as the box in Picnic Partner (page 53), you'll need a much stiffer, heavier weight of interfacing. Fusible interfacing, applied with an iron, works well on most fabrics. Avoid using it on velvet or corduroy, however, because the iron will crush the nap.

LAYERING AND STUFFING MATERIALS

Flannel, cotton batting, or fusible fleece provide a soft touch to any present that needs a cushioning layer between fabrics—like the Counting Sleep mask (page 73). When making pillows, you'll discover that precut foam forms in just the right size always fill the need. For stuffing shapes, polyester fiberfill is the all-around favorite material of choice . . . unless of course you decide to make the Patchwork Doorstop (page 50), which is literally full of beans.

FRAY RETARDANT

A product that binds with fibers to prevent unraveling, it comes in both liquid and spray-on applications. Use it when you find yourself in a tight spot, like when you're unable to zigzag a seam, or anytime you want to seal raw edges, as for appliqués.

BIAS TAPE

Bias tape is made from strips of fabric cut on the bias (diagonal) rather than the straight of the grain. This gives the tape the perfect amount of stretch for skirting corners and curves when binding raw edges. You can purchase single-fold or double-fold bias tape in various widths (blanket binding is extra wide) and in an almost infinite range of colors. To give your gift a custom look, make your own contrasting or coordinating bias tape (page 24). It's easy!

PIPING

Piping is a round trim you sew into a seam. You can make piping by wrapping a bias strip around a cord, then stitching close to the cord to hold it in place. Easier still, you can purchase packages of piping, which come in a range of fabrics, diameters, and colors.

HOOK-AND-LOOP TAPE

The story of hook-and-loop tape is truly a gripping tale. Exuding strength, yet ready to yield when stretched, it is *the* model of a perfect give-and-take relationship. The tape comes in many widths and, for your convenience, also comes in precut shapes, such as tabs or buttons.

RIBBONS, RICKRACK, AND TRIMS

It's amazing how much decorative impact you can make with little lengths of ribbon and trim. Whether in grosgrain, satin, or velvet, ribbon always dresses up your gifts. While novelty metallic trims add sparkle, a bit of lace trim can add either a touch of elegance or whimsy. Rickrack, that perennial wavy favorite, provides a fun way to add detail to designs or to finish edges.

ZIPPERS

You'll find several projects have zippered pockets—the Precious Cargo carryall (page 80) and the Undercover Portfolio (page 102), for example. Nylon zippers are less bulky than metal ones, especially for small gifts. Zippers come in a variety of lengths and are easy to apply using a standard straight application (page 26).

BUTTONS, EYELETS, AND SNAPS

Even though each of these small notions serves a purpose, they can do double duty as beautiful embellishments. In other words, why settle for plain when the world is full of fabulous decorative buttons? Same for snaps—in the time it takes to sew one, you could apply an even snappier version. And eyelets (also called grommets), those humble little metal circles, carry a drawstring with a bit more cachet than a buttonhole.

HARDWARE

D-rings, split rings (commonly called key rings), and magnets are essential bits of hardware when you're looking to make the right attachments. You can find these at craft or sewing stores or online.

MAGNETIC ATTRACTION

If your project includes magnets, like the Keep Your Place bookmarks (page 70), you'll need to know how to get out of a potentially sticky situation when you're sewing. Magnets are attracted to the machine's metal plate, which can slow down your stitching. If this happens, use a gentle, steady pressure to pull the fabric though the needle.

FUSIBLE WEB

Some inventions are truly a gift from the universe. This versatile no-sew alternative for affixing fabric to fabric uses a heat-activated adhesive for its sticky.

Paper-backed fusible web, much like double-sided tape, lets you adhere two surfaces, making it the perfect material for making and applying appliqués with ease (page 27).

FABRICS

If you've ever walked into a fabric store with your fingers twitching in anticipation of touching that first bolt, or if you've stood for hours deciding between the blue-green or green-blue, then you *really* love fabric and you know what it's all about. When you sew a gift to give, you're just sharing that love.

COTTON

Is there anything this fabric can't do? The different weights—from gossamer to canvas—fill many needs. Medium-weight cotton is suitable for making most of the presents in this book. It's easy to sew and comes in a wide variety of colors and patterns. Choose one you love.

SILK

Silk adds a touch of luxury and refinement to any present. Keep in mind that this fabric is sturdier than it looks. Since most of the gifts in this book are practical as well as pretty, choose medium- to heavy-weight silk; it will stand up to use. Silk has a tendency to ravel or fray, so take a little extra time to overcast any seams or raw edges.

UPHOLSTERY AND HOME DECORATING FABRICS

These fabrics are in a category all their own—but don't let that stop you. Even if you aren't covering a sofa or sewing drapes, you can still use these fabrics to make perfect little presents. The wide array of textures, colors, and patterns available in natural fibers, synthetics, and blends is worth a look.

WOOL

Classic and classy, wool endures as a favorite sewing fabric. Adding a small touch to a present provides texture and charm.

FELT

What's soft, doesn't ravel, has no right or wrong side, and is available for purchase in just about any store that carries sewing or craft supplies? Felt, of course. No wonder it's a crafter's favorite fabric. Traditionally, felt is made of wool, although the squares or bolts of felt you find in stores may be made from synthetic fibers.

RECYCLED KNITS

Who needs to know how to knit when you can reuse knitted fabric from an old scarf, sweater, or jersey? This stretchy fabric works well for covering odd shapes with ease, like the hanger in A Bird for All Seasons (page 44).

PHAT QUARTERS!

A fat quarter is a half-yard of fabric that has been cut in half to make a piece measuring 18 x 21 inches (45.7 x 53.3 cm). You may know them more commonly as those irresistible little bundles of colorful fabric you see at the shops. They're the perfect size for making small gifts, so buy an assortment.

FLEECE

Fleece is easy to sew and durable, as well as washable and quick-drying. But its biggest appeal is its inviting plush texture. Use it for cuddly baby gifts or whenever you want to make someone a present that feels like a hug.

VINYL

Clear vinyl is essential when making presents with see-through pockets or windows like the Happy Honeymoon luggage tags (page 98). You can purchase vinyl off the bolt at a fabric store, or you can trim a bit off an old clear vinyl tablecloth. (Just make sure no one's watching!)

LINEN

The word "crisp" comes to mind when we think of linen, as do the words "lustrous" and "beautiful." Use it when you need a durable fabric that has a bit of body to it. (Hint: It's a classic fabric for making napkins!) Linen does wrinkle, so iron it often before, during, and after sewing to keep it smooth.

SLICK TIP

If you find vinyl slipping and sliding through the presser foot as you stitch, look to the kitchen for your solution. Place a piece of wax paper over the vinyl, lower the presser foot, and sew. When you're finished, just tear the wax paper away from the stitching.

CHENILLE

Chenille's a super-soft, textured fabric that can be made from wool, cotton, silk, or rayon. It can make an already soft and friendly item into something deliciously cozy. Some chenille fabrics are more washable or fragile than others, so check out the details before you buy and test it before you sew.

STRETCH KNIT

Two clear advantages to stretch knit are that it's durable and has a lot of give. Generally made from polyester, cotton, and/or wool combined with spandex, stretch knits are widely available.

$presents$techniques

Unlike shaking a gift to try to find out what's inside, there's no guesswork here. This section contains the basic sewing know-how you'll need to make all the beautiful presents you want to give. If you're a beginner, use the section to learn something new. For those more experienced, treat yourself to a quick review. That way you'll know what to expect, and can get right to work.

MACHINE STITCHING

First, test the tension of your machine by stitching on a scrap of the fabric you'll be using; you want the stitches to be smooth on both sides. If necessary, follow the instructions in your machine's manual to adjust the tension for the top thread or the bobbin. When you're ready, follow these steps to sew the perfect seam.

1 Pin the fabric pieces together using straight pins placed at right angles to the seam. Unless the project instructions tell you otherwise, most seams are sewn with right sides together and raw edges aligned.

2 As you sew, pull the pins out *before* they reach the needle. Be quick! If you're too late, the machine needle can nick the pins, which will dull it, or—worse—the pins can break the needle.

3 Pivoting the fabric when sewing a corner will give you a perfect sharp angle. When you get to the corner point, stop with the needle down in the fabric. Then lift the presser foot, turn the fabric, lower the presser foot, and merrily sew on your way.

4 Give it up! Let the machine do the work of pulling the fabric through as you sew. This simple exercise can save you uneven stitches, stretched fabric, and puckered seams.

CLIPPING CORNERS

When you turn a corner right side out, the excess fabric can bunch in the seams, creating ugly lumps and bumps. But don't worry. A few well-placed snips and clips can smooth your work to perfection.

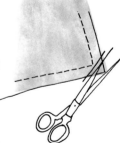

figure 1

After sewing, cut the seam allowance at a 45° angle to the raw edge. Cut close to the stitching, but be careful to avoid cutting the stitches (figure 1).

CLIPPING OR NOTCHING CURVES

Just like corners, sewn curves need some attention, too. You clip an inward curve but notch an outward one. To clip an inward curve, use scissors to cut into the seam allowance at several places around the curve (figure 2). Don't clip too close since you don't want to cut into the stitching. To notch an outward curve, cut small v-shaped wedges from the seam allowance (figure 3), being careful to avoid cutting into the stitching.

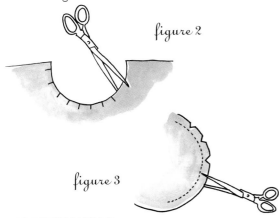

figure 2

figure 3

TOPSTITCHING

In this technique, you sew a line of stitching on the right side of the fabric that runs parallel to the edge or seam. Topstitching can be purely decorative, but it has a practical side, too, such as when you need to flatten a seam or keep a lining in place.

EDGESTITCHING

Edgestitching is simply topstitching that hugs the edge of a seam. Make it the same way as topstitching, except sew as close to the edge as possible.

MAKING AND ATTACHING STRAPS

A strap handle, like the one in the Nesting Instinct tote (page 116), is quick and easy to make and attach. Start with a straight strip of fabric. Fold the two long raw edges under, wrong sides together, to make narrow hems, and press (figure 4). Fold the strip in half lengthwise, aligning the edges, and press in the crease. Topstitch both long sides of the strap (figure 5). (Don't forget to make two!) Pin the right sides of the strap to the right sides of the bag (figure 6), and you're ready to sew them into the seam of the binding or lining.

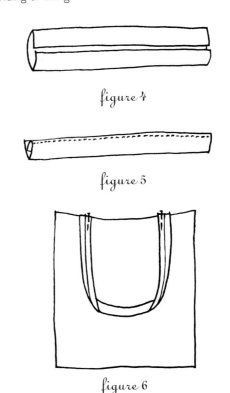

figure 4

figure 5

figure 6

BINDING WITH BIAS TAPE

Bias tape binds raw edges for a finished look. To bind around an edge with curves, as for the Counting Sleep mask (page 73), follow the instructions for Binding a Circumference below. When you have a project that has straight edges and corners, such as the Pocket Placemats (page 58), follow the instructions for Binding with Mitered Corners (page 23).

BINDING A CIRCUMFERENCE

1 Measure the length of the edge you want to bind, and then add an extra couple inches for folding under the raw ends. Cut the tape to this length.

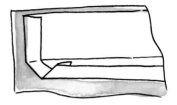

figure 7

2 Open the tape and fold one of the ends under (figure 7). With right sides together, pin the tape to the fabric with raw edges aligned. Sew the layers together, using the crease in the tape as the guide for the seam allowance.

3 Stop stitching 3 inches (7.6 cm) from your starting point. Fold the other loose end under to overlap the stitched tape by 1 inch (2.5 cm) (figure 8). You may need to trim the loose end before folding to reduce the bulk. Complete stitching the seam.

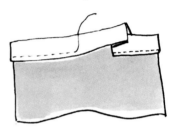

figure 8

4 Fold the bias tape over the seam allowance to the other side of the fabric and pin it in place. Slipstitch by hand to secure it (figure 9). Alternatively, you can edgestitch so the stitching hardly shows. Just make sure the edgestitching catches the binding on the back (figure 10).

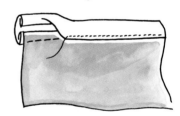

figure 9

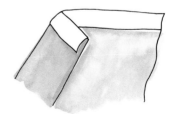

figure 10

BINDING WITH MITERED CORNERS

1 Measure the length of the edge to bind, and then add an extra couple inches for folding under the raw ends and overlapping.

2 As you did in step 2 of Binding a Circumference (page 22), open the tape and fold one of the ends under. With right sides together and raw edges aligned, sew the tape to the fabric. Stop sewing ¼ inch (6 mm) from the corner, and then fold the binding over itself to create a crease (figure 11).

3 Fold the binding down and rotate the fabric 90°. Don't stitch across the corner, but instead stitch ¼ inch (6 mm) in from the edge (figure 12), sewing down toward the next corner. Continue stitching around the edges and mitering the corners in this way until you get back to your starting point.

4 Fold the loose end under to overlap the starting point by 1 inch (2.5 cm), trimming the end first if necessary to reduce the bulk. Then complete stitching the seam. Fold the binding over the seam allowance to the other side of the fabric. Fold the edges of the corners in as you would if wrapping a package (figure 13), and then slipstitch the binding to the other side of the fabric.

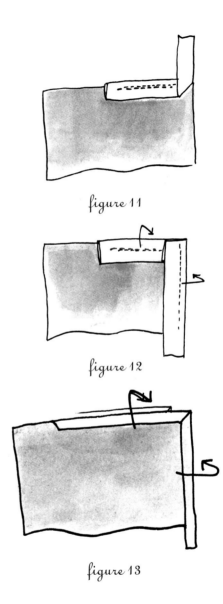

figure 11

figure 12

figure 13

MAKING BIAS TAPE

To get a coordinated, custom look, make your own bias tape. It's easier than you might think, and it adds sew much more to every gift.

1 Cut strips four times as wide as your desired tape on lines running 45° to the selvage (figure 14).

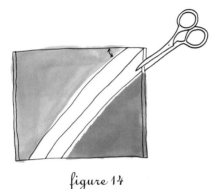

figure 14

2 Piece the strips by laying one strip over another, with right sides together and at right angles. Pin them together, and then stitch diagonally across the corners of the overlapping squares (figure 15). Cut off the corners, leaving a ¼-inch (6 mm) seam allowance.

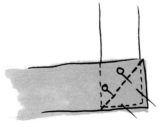

figure 15

3 Open the seams and press the seam allowances flat. Fold the strip in half lengthwise, wrong sides together, and press again. Open the strip and press the raw edges into the center. This makes single-fold bias tape (figure 16).

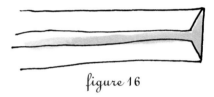

figure 16

4 To make double-fold bias tape, fold the strip into the center again and press (figure 17).

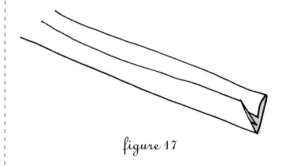

figure 17

ADDING A LINING

If your gift calls for a lining, think of it as double the opportunity to use more great fabric. The Hold Anything boxes (page 38) use a method of turned lining that is common when making open-top purses:

1 Every lining has a back and a front piece; some may have a bottom piece as well. Stitch the lining pieces together with right sides facing. Leave an opening at the bottom for turning (figure 18). Trim the seams and press them open. Don't turn the lining, but leave it wrong side out.

2 Slip the lining over the bag, right sides together. Line up the seams and top edges, and then pin them down. If the bag has straps, make sure they are in between the fabrics—you don't want them getting caught in the seam allowance. Stitch the seam, trim it, and clip the curves.

3 Turn the bag through the opening (figure 19). Stitch the opening closed by hand or machine. Push the lining into the bag before pressing the top edge.

A second lining method uses a simple drop-in lining:

1 Sew your lining with right sides together. Clip the corners and trim the seam allowances. Press the seams and clip any curves. Turn the lining right side out.

2 Slip the lining into the bag, wrong sides together. Align the seams and raw edges, and then pin it in place. The bag is now ready to finish according to the instructions.

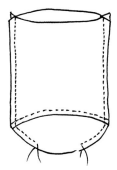

figure 18

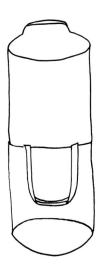

figure 19

PIECING

If you prefer a bit of patchwork, consider making the Take Note book cover (page 32) or the Patchwork Doorstop (page 50). For perfect piecing, start by pinning the first two squares or rectangles, right sides together. Stitch along the edge using the desired seam allowance. Add more pieces in the same way to make a row. When one row is complete, make another. Then pin and sew the rows together.

QUILTING

Quilting creates a padded, textured fabric, which is both practical and decorative. You make it by sandwiching batting between two layers of fabric, and then stitching the layers together by machine or by hand, using a running stitch (page 29). Before stitching, place pins or sew long basting stitches to hold the layers together to prevent them from shifting.

INSTALLING ZIPPERS

The simplest of centered straight applications is all you'll need when making Precious Cargo (page 80), Passport, Please (page 66), or Undercover Portfolio (page 102). The project instructions will provide their own variations on the following steps.

1 Fold the seam allowance under each side and press. If you're sewing the zipper to vinyl or ribbon, there's no need to fold and press it.

2 Lay the closed zipper right side up. Add the fabric, right side up, lining up the seam, one side at a time. Pin or baste it down (figure 20).

3 Use a zipper foot for sewing. Start at the top on one side of the zipper, and sew down through all layers. When you reach the end of the zipper, pivot the fabric in the machine, and sew across the bottom. Then pivot again to turn the fabric, and sew up the other side.

figure 20

EMBELLISHING

Sometimes it's the littlest touches that add the most to sewn presents. Add embellishments as a signature to personalize a gift, and you will charm any recipient.

MAKING YO-YOS

"Yo-yo" is another (and much more fun) name for a gathered rosette. Its slightly puffy texture makes it a perfect fabric embellishment. Here's how to make one:

1 Determine the diameter measurement of the finished yo-yo. Measure twice that plus ½ inch (1.3 cm) and cut out a circle of that diameter.

2 Stitch a ¼-inch (6 mm) hem around the perimeter of the circle. You'll get better results if you fold as you sew rather than pressing in the hem (figure 21).

3 Gently pull one thread to gather the edges to the center (figure 22). Secure the gathered center with a few stitches. Then knot and trim the thread. Use your hand to flatten the yo-yo—never use an iron.

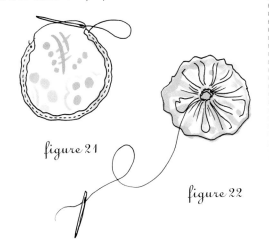

figure 21

figure 22

ATTACHING APPLIQUÉS

Fabric cutouts add texture and visual interest to a design. You can sew them on by hand or machine. One of the quickest ways to apply appliqués is to use lightweight paper-backed fusible web (page 17) to fix them to the fabric.

1 Apply the fusible web to the fabric following the manufacturer's instructions. Do not remove the paper backing. Draw or trace the outline of the appliqué directly on the paper, then cut it out. (Because you're working on the wrong side of the fabric, the design you draw will appear in reverse when you apply it.)

2 Remove the paper backing. Position the appliqué on your fabric, and press it with an iron according to the instructions.

3 You can finish the edges of the appliqué to keep it from raveling by using either a hand or machine stitch. Fray retardant (page 15), applied before affixing the appliqué, will also prevent raveling.

DESIGN AT YOUR FINGERTIPS

When thinking embellishment, don't forget your sewing machine's selection of decorative stitches. With a twist of a knob, you can add new direction to your design.

HAND STITCHES

Sooner or later, you'll have to abandon your machine and take up needle and thread (or floss). The following are descriptions of the most common stitches you'll need for the projects in this book.

APPLIQUÉ STITCH

Done right, these tiny stitches are practically invisible. Use them when stitching on an appliqué. Poke the needle through the base fabric and up through the appliqué. Bring the needle down into the base fabric just a bit away and repeat.

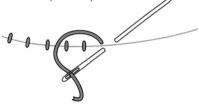

BACKSTITCH

The backstitch is a basic method for creating a seam that works well for holding seams under pressure. It can also be used to outline shapes or text.

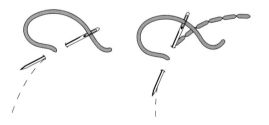

BLANKET STITCH

The blanket stitch is both decorative and functional. Use this stitch to accentuate an edge or to attach an appliqué.

CHAIN STITCH

You can make this stitch in a circle or following a line to create a flower.

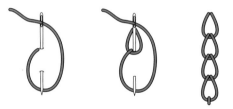

FRENCH KNOT

This elegant little knot adds interest and texture when embroidering or embellishing.

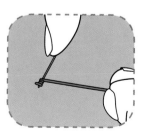

RUNNING STITCH

Make this stitch by weaving the needle through the fabric at evenly spaced intervals.

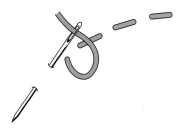

SLIPSTITCH

This stitch is perfect for closing seams. Slip the needle through one end of the open seam to anchor the thread, and then take a small stitch through the fold, pulling the needle through. In the other side of the seam, insert the needle directly opposite the stitch you just made, and take a stitch through the fold. Repeat.

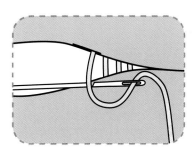

SPLIT STITCH

Make a first stitch. For the second stitch, bring the needle up through the middle of the first stitch, splitting it. Then follow the line, with the needle coming up through the working thread and splitting it.

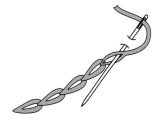

WHIPSTITCH

The whipstitch is used to bind two edges together. Sew the stitches over the edge of the fabric.

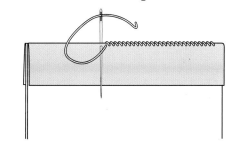

host(ess) with the most(est)

You're guaranteed a return visit when you give your host one of these precious presents.

take note

𝒩eed a gift for a hostess who likes to travel or keep a journal? Here's the perfect solution: a stylish notebook cover with a hint of Asian flavor. Your lucky friend won't leave home without it.

DESIGNER

LISA COX

WHAT YOU NEED

Basic Presents Tool Kit (page 11)

¼ yard (22.9 cm) or one fat quarter of Japanese navy print cotton

¼ yard (22.9 cm) or one fat quarter of plain flannel

6 scrap pieces of indigo and white Asian-inspired cotton, each between 2 x 1 inch (5.1 x 2.5 cm) and 2 x 2 inches (5.1 x 5.1 cm)

Textured navy cotton, 7 x 14 inches (17.8 x 35.6 cm)

Cotton thread in white

Chopstick or knitting needle

¾-inch (1.9 cm) navy grosgrain ribbon, 9½ inches (24.1 cm) in length

Japanese coin with center hole or Japanese-themed button

Black sew-in hook and loop tape, ¾ inch (1.9 cm) square

Small wooden bead

Purchased notebook, 4 x 6 inches (10.2 x 15.2 cm)

SEAM ALLOWANCE

¼ inch (6 mm)

WHAT YOU DO

1 From the Japanese print cotton, cut five pieces: one at 7 x 14 inches (17.8 x 35.6 cm); two at 1½ x 2 inches (3.8 x 5.1 cm); and two at 3¾ x 1½ inches (9.5 x 3.8 cm).

2 From the flannel, cut three pieces: one at 7 x 14 inches (17.8 x 35.6 cm); another at 1½ x 2 inches (3.8 x 5.1 cm); and one at 3¾ x 1½ inches (9.5 x 3.8 cm).

3 Sew the six pieces of Asian fabric together to form a strip that's 2 x 7 inches (5.1 x 17.8 cm). Press the seam allowances in one direction.

4 Place the textured navy fabric face up on your worktable. Draw a vertical line 4 inches (10.2 cm) from the right side. Draw another line 1½ inches (3.8 cm) to the left of the first line. Using the rotary cutter, remove the strip between the lines. Sew the patchwork strip to the cover fabric, right sides facing, and press seam allowances out.

5 Draw a vertical line ⅜ inch (1 cm) on either side of the strip. Using the white thread, sew a small running stitch along the lines.

6 To make the bookmark tab, layer the two 1½ x 2-inch (3.8 x 5.1 cm) pieces of Japanese print cotton with right sides together. Place the same-size piece of flannel on top. Sew around both long sides and one short side. Clip the corners and turn it right side out, using the chopstick to poke out the corners. Turn the open seam under and press.

7 Insert one end of the ribbon, center it, and topstitch around the whole tab, ⅛ inch (3 mm) from the edge. Pin the other end of the ribbon to the top center of the textured navy fabric and baste it in place, ⅛ inch (3 mm) from the edge.

8 Layer the large flannel piece, the large piece of quilting fabric (right side up), and the *(continued on next page)*

textured navy fabric (right side down). Pin them together and then sew around all four sides, leaving a 3-inch (7.6 cm) gap on a short edge for turning. Do not sew over the bookmark. Clip the corners and turn it right side out. Turn the open seam under ¼ inch (6 mm) and press. Topstitch ⅛ inch (3 mm) from the edge along both short ends.

9 Place the remaining piece of flannel under the other two like-sized fabric pieces, right sides together. Cut one short end into a rounded shape, using the button as a template. Sew around the two long ends and the rounded end. Clip the curves, turn it right side out, and press. Turn the open end under ¼ inch (6 mm) and press.

10 Sew the loop side of the hook and loop tape underneath the rounded end of the strip completed in step 9. Sew the Japanese coin or button to the reverse side with the white thread, using the wooden bead to keep it in place. Position the hook side of the hook and loop tape 1½ inches (3.8 cm) from the top of the notebook cover, near the

white stitching (see the project photo). Sew it in place.

11 Fold a 2-inch (5.1 cm) flap on each end of the notebook cover and pin in place close to the edge. Slide the notebook into the cover to ensure a good fit, adjusting as necessary. Decide where to place the tab on the rear of the notebook cover so it matches the piece on the front.

Stitch in place securely, sewing in an "X" pattern.

12 Using a denim or topstitching needle in the sewing machine, topstitch along the top and bottom edges of the notebook cover, ⅛ inch (3 mm) from the edge, securing the flaps in place.

sew convenient

*I*f you have a friend who brings sewing projects with her wherever she goes—on vacation, in the car, or at the soccer game—she will adore this little gift. It will get her up and sewing in no time!

DESIGNER

KATHERINE ACCETTURA

WHAT YOU NEED

Basic Presents Tool Kit (page 11)

Patterns (page 128)

Fabric for the inner shell,
10 x 10 inches (25.4 x 25.4 cm)

Fabric for the outer shell,
10 x 10 inches (25.4 x 25.4 cm)

Cotton batting or fleece for
padding, 10 x 10 inches
(25.4 x 25.4 cm)

Coordinating wool or acrylic felt,
7 x 7 inches (17.8 x 17.8 cm)

Hook-and-loop tape, about 1 inch
(2.5 cm) long

Coordinating shank button, small
to medium in size

WHAT YOU DO

1 Using the large pattern, cut one shape each from the inner fabric, the outer fabric, and the batting or fleece. Using the small pattern, cut one shape from the felt.

2 Layer the large pieces from bottom to top: the batting/fleece, the inner fabric (right side up), and the outer fabric (right side down). Pin the layers together on all sides.

3 Using a small stitch, sew ¼ inch (6 mm) from the edge all the way around, leaving a 1-inch (2.5 cm) gap to turn the layers right side out. Stop after sewing each arch and pivot the needle while raising the presser foot (see page 20 for more machine-sewing instructions). Emphasize the curves during this step if possible.

4 Trim the edges to reduce the seam allowance. Clip tiny notches into the edges (page 21) so the shape will remain flat and round when turned right side out.

5 Flip the fabric right side out through the gap. Press it flat with the iron. Hand sew the gap closed and then topstitch close to the edge all the way around.

6 Pin the felt piece to the center of the inner fabric, aligning the contours of the arches. Use at least four pins. Sew through all layers from the dip between each arch into the center (refer to the pattern on page 128).

7 Cut the hook-and-loop tape so it fits on the tab's underside. Make sure you can't see it from the top of the tab. Pin it in place and sew closely around the edges.

8 Fold up the fabric piece by bunching the arches together so they touch, collapsing on the center (figure 1). Line up the arches as much as possible. Fold down the tab to see where to affix the other side of the hook-and-loop tape. Mark the spot on the outer fabric and sew it down.

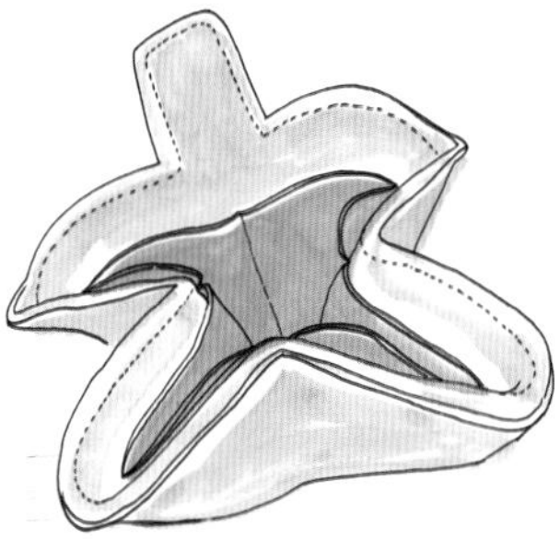

9 Affix the shank button to the top of the tab. Now wherever you (or your friends) go, you can safely travel with sewing needles.

figure 1

NEEDLING PERSONALITY

You may choose to do some decorative stitching as well. Give this gift your own personal touch; your friends will notice.

hold anything

DESIGNER

CELINE REID

$\mathcal{P}$art of the fun of receiving these stylish containers is counting all the rooms in the house where they could come in handy. As a bonus, you can fill them with additional gifts before you wrap them up!

WHAT YOU NEED

Basic Presents Tool Kit (page 11)

⅓ yard (30.5 cm) of medium-weight fabric (e.g., upholstery fabric or heavy linen)

⅓ yard (30.5 cm) of printed cotton fabric

SEAM ALLOWANCE

⅜ inch (1 cm)

WHAT YOU DO

1 Cut two 10½ x 9-inch (26.7 x 22.9 cm) rectangles in the medium-weight fabric. Cut a circle with a 6¾-inch (17.1 cm) diameter. These pieces make the outer fabric of the box. Repeat with the printed cotton to fashion the inner fabric.

2 Pin the outer fabric rectangles together, right sides facing, and straight-stitch along each short side. Repeat with the inner fabric, except sew only one short side completely. On the other short side, sew about 3 inches (7.6 cm), leave a 4-inch (10.2 cm) gap, and then sew to the end.

3 Pin the outer fabric circle to a short side of the outer fabric rectangles, right sides together, and sew all around. Repeat with the inner fabric, using the fully sewn short side as the base.

4 Insert the inner box into the outer box, right sides together. Sew the two boxes together at the top edge.

5 Turn the box right side out through the opening. Close the opening with a straight stitch.

6 Shape the box by stuffing the inner fabric inside the outer fabric. To finish, topstitch along the top edge. Turn the top of the box out, and it's ready to use.

BOTH SIDES NOW

If you make this project with heavy-duty fabrics—ones that will stand up to heavy use—the box is completely reversible. Make a few and turn one inside out to make a decorative statement.

in the bag

Ah, the gift of wine: it's personal, tasteful, and so convenient. But don't just hand over a bottle. You want your friends to unwrap it and savor it. This little present fits the bill ... and the bottle.

DESIGNER

JOAN K. MORRIS

WHAT YOU NEED

Basic Presents Tool Kit (page 11)

Wine Bottle

¼ yard (22.9 cm) of pink microfiber fabric

¼ yard (22.9 cm) of polka dot cotton blend fabric

Thread in off white and pink

2 silver eyelets, ¼ inch (6 mm) in diameter

Eyelet setter

Large safety pin

Pink cord, 24 inches (6 cm) in length

2-inch (5,1 cm) orange buckle

1½ -inch (3.8 cm) wide ribbon, 18 inches (45.7 cm) in length

SEAM ALLOWANCE

½ inch (1.3 cm)

WHAT YOU DO

1 On scrap paper, trace the bottom of the bottle. Add 1 inch (2.5 cm) around and cut it out. Use it to cut out a circle of the microfiber fabric.

2 Cut a rectangle of microfiber to 5 x 13 inches (12.7 x 33 cm). Cut a 13-inch (33 cm) square of the polka dot fabric. Pin them, right sides facing, along the long edge. Machine-stitch them together, pressing the seam toward the polka dot fabric. Topstitch ¼ inch (6 mm) from the seam.

3 Fold down the top edge of the polka dot fabric 4½ inches (11.4 cm). Press. Turn the edge under ¼ inch (4 mm) and press again. Machine-stitch close to the edge.

4 Measure 3 inches (7.6 cm) down from the top fold and 1½ inches (3.8 cm) in from each edge. Mark the spots. Set eyelets at each point through only the top layer of fabric.

5 To make a casing, measure 2½ inches (6.4 cm) down from the top edge and stitch a line across. Stitch another line 1 inch (2.5 cm) below the first, centering the eyelets between the lines. Use the safety pin to run the cord through the casing from eyelet to eyelet.

6 Center the buckle on the ribbon. Pin them to the front of the bag, 5 inches (12.7 cm) down from the top edge. Machine-stitch the top ribbon edge in place. Stitch as close as you can to the buckle. Turn and stitch across the ribbon and back along the bottom edge. Repeat on the other side.

7 Pin the fabric circle to the bottom edge of the bag, wrong sides together. Starting ½ inch (1.3 cm) from the side, stitch around the bottom, easing the circle as you go. At the starting point, ½ inch (1.3 cm) of fabric remains to form the side seam. Clip the curves (figure 1). Machine-stitch the side seam with a zigzag stitch. Then trim it. Press the seam to one side. Add a light zigzag stitch to hold the seam.

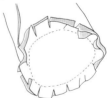

figure 1

8 Turn the bag right side out and push out the bottom. Center the cord around the neck and tie a loose single knot. Knot the two ends together. Loosen the knot, slide in the bottle, and tighten the knot again.

all buttoned up

𝒯he four napkin rings in this clever project are easy to make, and you can add your own personal touches by matching fabric and button … or go against the grain and make four different ones.

DESIGNER

ROXANNE BEAUVAIS

WHAT YOU NEED

Basic Presents Tool Kit (page 11)

Pattern (page 128)

¼ yard (22.9 cm) of cotton fabric (one fat quarter)

10-inch (25.4 cm) square of medium-weight sew-in interfacing

3 spools of thread: one matching the color of the fabric, one contrasting color, and one matching the color of the buttons

Iron-on hook-and-loop tape

4 buttons, ¼ inch (1.9 cm) or smaller

WHAT YOU DO

1. Cut out eight pattern pieces from the cotton fabric and four from the interfacing.

2. Layer two fabric pieces, right sides together. Place one piece of interfacing on top. Sew around the shape, leaving the needle down when you rotate the fabric to create a smooth curve. Leave a 2-inch (5.1 cm) opening along a straight edge to turn the ring right side out.

3. Notch the seam allowance on both curves, and then turn the ring right side out. Use the blunt end of the pencil to push out the curves. Press well.

4. Using the contrasting thread, top stitch around the entire ring ¼ inch (6 mm) from the edge. This will also close the 2-inch (5.1 cm) opening.

5. Fold the ring in half lengthwise and mark the center. Starting at this center point, sew straight lines the long way, ¼ inch (6 mm) apart, to create a modern quilted pattern (see the photo below). Pull the threads through to one side, tie a knot, and clip the threads.

6. Iron on a 1-inch (2.5 cm) square of hook-and-loop tape in the position marked on the pattern. Apply the loop side to the bottom and the hook side to the top.

7. Hand sew a button on the top right-hand side of the cuff, opposite the hook-and-loop tape so that when closed, the button sits on the outside over the hook-and-loop tape.

8. Repeat steps 2 through 7 for additional rings.

a bird for all seasons

𝒯his present gives you a two-fer: The fabric-wrapped hanger will delight, but the dangling sachet bird will surprise. She'll keep clothes smelling fresh on and off the hanger.

DESIGNER

FIONA HESFORD

WHAT YOU NEED

Basic Presents Tool Kit (page 11)

Patterns (page 127)

Padded clothes hanger, about 17 inches (43.2 cm) wide

2 pieces of knitted striped fabric, 6 x 6 inches (15.2 x 15.2 cm) and 5 x 17 inches (12.7 x 43.2 cm)

2 pieces of ribbon, one lilac and one blue-and-white gingham, each 12 inches (30.5 cm) long

Craft glue

Square of fusible and dissolvable stabilizer, 6 inches (15.2 cm) to a side

2 squares of felt in white and lilac, about 4 inches (10.2 cm) to a side

Small scraps of brown and orange felt

1 ounce of dried lavender

2 buttons, ⅜ inch (1 cm)

Black sewing thread

Plastic kitchen funnel (optional)

SEAM ALLOWANCE

¼ inch (6 mm), unless otherwise noted

WHAT YOU DO

MAKING THE HANGER

1 Unscrew the metal hook from the hanger and set it aside.

2 Fold the larger piece of knitted fabric in half lengthwise with right sides together. Sew around the edges, leaving one narrow end open. Round off the edges by sewing across the corners.

3 Turn it inside out. Push the hanger into the knitted tube and sew up the open end by hand.

4 Replace the metal hook. Tie a tight lilac ribbon bow around the hook. Fix it in place with a blob of glue.

MAKING THE BIRD

5 Iron on the fusible stabilizer to the wrong side of the knitted fabric square. Using Template A, copy one bird shape on the wrong side of the knit and one on the wrong side of the white felt. Cut them out.

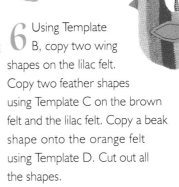

6 Using Template B, copy two wing shapes on the lilac felt. Copy two feather shapes using Template C on the brown felt and the lilac felt. Copy a beak shape onto the orange felt using Template D. Cut out all the shapes.

7 Pin and sew the wings to the right side of both bird shapes. Turn the knit bird shape right side down, and pin the beak in place, sticking out past the front of the bird head (see the project photograph). Pin the ends of the ribbon to the middle of the bird's back.

8 Leaving a 2-inch (5.1 cm) opening at the base, baste together the two bird shapes, right sides facing. Sew around the edges. Trim the seams and nick the curved edges.

9 Turn it right side out and fill the bird with the lavender. Sew up the opening by hand. Attach the button eyes with black thread and add the felt feathers at the tail.

welcome home

Someone you know has a new
home with everything they need—
except a perfect little gift made
just for them.

leaf it alone trivet

DESIGNER

CANDACE TODD

*P*ractical yet personal, this pretty little gift belongs in everyone's kitchen. Use the leaf template provided or create your own motif. Either way, your recipient will love it.

WHAT YOU NEED

Basic Presents Tool Kit (page 11)

Leaf pattern (page 127)

¼ yard (22.9 cm) linen fabric

Batting

Embroidery needle

Embroidery thread

Fusible webbing

3 patterned fabric scraps,
3 x 4 inches (7.6 x 10.2 cm)

SEAM ALLOWANCE

¼ inch (6 mm)

WHAT YOU DO

1 Cut out two squares of linen and one square of batting, each 8 inches (20.3 cm) per side. Layer the linen, right sides together, and then place the batting on top. Sew around the edges, leaving a 3-inch (7.6 cm) opening centered on one side.

2 Notch the corners and turn the trivet right side out, holding the batting and one piece of linen as if they were one piece. Push out the corners.

3 Iron the edges flat and fold in the raw edges of the opening. Pin it closed and topstitch completely around the trivet.

4 Hand-quilt the trivet using the embroidery thread. Push the needle through the top layer of fabric and the batting, but not through the bottom layer of fabric. Pull the needle out where you want to start stitching. Give the thread a little tug, and the knot should disappear into the fabric. Snip off any excess thread from the first stitch.

5 Quilt from side to side using a running stitch. Sew through all layers. When you tie off the thread, bury it in the batting as you did in step 4.

6 Iron the fusible webbing to the back of the fabric scraps. Trace two leaf patterns onto each scrap and then cut them out. Remove the paper backing, position the leaves on the trivet, and then iron them into place. Topstitch around each leaf twice.

patchwork doorstop

DESIGNER

ELIZABETH HARTMAN

*F*or the friend who has everything else: a quilted doorstop. Once you create its nine-block design, it might even be too pretty to hide on the floor.

WHAT YOU NEED

Basic Presents Tool Kit (page 11)

Scraps of wool suiting: 2 strips, each 5½ x 3¼ inches (14 x 8.3 cm); 2 strips, each 10 x 3¼ inches (25.4 x 8.3 cm); and 1 strip, 2½ x 9 inches (6.4 x 22.9 cm)

Strip of lightweight fusible interfacing, 2½ x 9 inches (6.4 x 22.9 cm)

Scraps of printed cotton: one 10-inch (25.4 cm) square; one strip, 2½ x 9 inches (6.4 x 22.9 cm); and nine 2½-inch (6.4 cm) squares

Two 10-inch (25.4 cm) squares of fusible fleece

Zipper, 7 inches (17.8 cm) in length

Decorative plastic button

4–5 pounds of dried beans

SEAM ALLOWANCE

½ inch (1.3 cm)

WHAT YOU DO

1 Fuse the interfacing to the matching strip of wool suiting. Fold and press the long sides of the strip into the center, wrong sides together. Repeat with the 2½ x 9-inch (6.4 x 22.9 cm) scrap of cotton. Layer the two strips, wrong sides together, and stitch close to both long edges. Set the handle aside.

2 Iron one square of fusible fleece to the wrong side of the 10-inch (25.4 cm) cotton square. Machine-quilt in any pattern you want. Then pick one edge as the bottom and press it under ½ inch (1.3 cm), wrong sides together.

3 Arrange the nine 2½-inch (6.4 cm) cotton squares on a work surface. Stitch the squares together into three rows of three. Press the seams open and pin the rows together, lining up the seams, and then stitch the three rows into a nine-patch block. Press the seams open again.

4 Sew the 5½ x 3¼-inch (14 x 8.3 cm) wool suiting strips to the top and bottom of the patch block. Press the seams open. Then sew the 10 x 3¼-inch (25.4 x 8.3 cm) wool suiting strips to the left and right sides of the block. Again, press the seams open. Trim any uneven edges so the block is 10 inches (25.4 cm) square.

5 Iron the last square of fusible fleece to the wrong side of the block. Machine-quilt as desired. Press the bottom edge under ½ inch (1.3 cm), wrong sides together.

6 Pin the zipper to the center of the folded bottom edge of the front panel. Using a zipper foot, slowly stitch the zipper to the panel, removing pins as you go. Pin the other side of the zipper to the folded bottom edge of the back panel and sew it in place the same way. Open the zipper about 7 inches (17.8 cm) and keep it open for now.

7 With right sides together, pin the front and back panels along the top edge. Sew the two panels together. Press open the seam. Pin and sew the side seams, clipping the corners and pressing open the seams.

8 Measure and mark a ½-inch (1.3 cm) square at each corner. Trim the corners along these lines.

9 Starting at the bottom corner with the zipper's metal base (not the pull), open up the corner and stack the right side of the bottom seam on the right side of the side seam. Pin and stitch them together. If you've centered the zipper, the seam falls just outside the zipper base. Repeat at the opposite bottom corner.

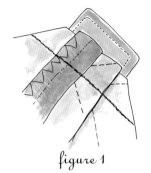

figure 1

10 Thread the whole handle through the top corner openings with the printed side facing the right side. Press one corner as you did the bottom corners, but keep the handle end threaded through. Stitch the corner closed, catching the handle (figure 1).

11 Repeat with the other top corner, making sure the handle isn't pulled too tight or left too loose. Trim the handle ends so they are even with the corner seams. Reinforce all four corner seams with several rows of zigzag stitching.

12 Turn the doorstop right side out. Sew the button on the center square of the patch block. Then fill the doorstop with the dried beans.

QUILT MARKS

You can use any quilt pattern you like, but the designer sewed a 1¼-inch (3.2 cm) diamond pattern. She measured it out with a quilting ruler and used a disappearing ink marker on the fabric as a guide (although masking tape also works well).

picnic partner

Linen and absorbent cotton make wonderful napkins, and a complementary fabric box stores them away neatly until the next time you dine under the sun or stars.

WHAT YOU NEED

Basic Presents Tool Kit (page 11)

1¼ yards (114.3 cm) of printed fabric

1¼ yards (114.3 cm) of linen

Embroidery hoop

Embroidery needle

One skein of embroidery thread to match printed fabric

Sewing thread to match embroidery thread

¼ yard (22.9 cm) of heavyweight interfacing

1 yard (91.4 cm) of matching ribbon or fabric strip, ½ inch (1.3 cm) wide

DESIGNER

STEPHANIE COSTO

WHAT YOU DO

MAKING THE NAPKINS

1 Cut six 13-inch (33 cm) squares of the print fabric. (If you're using two separate prints, cut three squares of each.) Cut six more 13-inch (33 cm) squares of the linen.

2 With the fabric pen, write initials (such as those of the planned recipient) at the bottom right corner of each piece of linen. Place one piece in the embroidery hoop and embroider over the initials, using a backstitch and six strands of embroidery thread in a color that matches the print fabric. Repeat for the remaining five linen pieces.

3 Place one linen and one printed fabric square right sides together. Sew the sides using a ½-inch (1.3 cm) seam allowance,

leaving a 2-inch (5.1 cm) opening on one side. Trim the seam and clip the corners, being careful not to clip through the stitching. Turn the fabric right side out and press the fabric so the seams lie flat.

4 Using a thread color that matches the embroidery, top stitch around all sides of the square, ¼ inch (6 mm) from the edge, making sure to close the opening.

5 Repeat steps 3 and 4 to make the remaining five napkins.

MAKING THE NAPKIN BOX

6 Cut a 13½-inch (34.3 cm) square from the printed fabric. Cut a 3¼-inch (8.3 cm) square out of each corner.

7 Fold each corner together along the cut, right sides together. Pin and sew the edges using a ½-inch (1.3 cm) seam allowance (figure 1). Trim the seams.

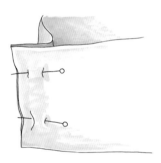

figure 1

8 Repeat steps 6 and 7 with the linen fabric, except for two things: fold the corners wrong sides together and leave a 1½-inch opening in one of the corners.

YOUR PRINT IS SHOWING

If you decide to use only one printed fabric, get the full amount (1¼ yards [114.3 cm]). If, however, you want to use two different printed fabrics, get ¾ yard (68.6 cm) of one and ½ yard (45.7 cm) of another.

9 Place the printed fabric inside the linen fabric so the right sides are together and the raw edges on top are even. Sew the fabrics together on the top raw edge using a ½-inch (1.3 cm) seam allowance. Trim the seams. Turn the fabric box right side out through the opening. Press the top edges to make the seam lie flat.

10 Cut a 6-inch (15.2 cm) piece of heavyweight interfacing. Roll it into a narrow tube and carefully insert it into the opening in the fabric box. Guide the interfacing so it lies flat on the bottom of the box.

11 Cut four 6 x 3¼-inch (15.2 x 8.3 cm) pieces of heavyweight interfacing. Using a wide zigzag stitch, sew the short sides together to form a four-sided box.

12 Roll the stitched sides into a long narrow tube. Insert it into the opening in the fabric box. Guide the sides of the heavyweight interfacing into the sides of the fabric box, matching up the corners. Press down the corners inside the box with your fingers.

13 Using a ¼-inch (6 mm) seam allowance and the thread color you used to top-stitch the fabric napkins, topstitch all around the top of the box. Slipstitch the opening by hand to close it.

PUTTING IT ALL TOGETHER

14 Fold each napkin into a 6-inch (15.2 cm) square and place it into the napkin box.

15 Tie a bow around the napkin box using the ribbon or fabric strip.

i ♥ you coasters

DESIGNER

WENDY ARACICH

You can whip up these adorable coasters in a jiffy if you need a last-minute gift. Use fabric remnants you have on hand to tailor the coasters to your friend's style or décor.

WHAT YOU NEED

Basic Presents Tool Kit (page 11)

Pink felt, ¼ yard (22.9 cm)

Black-and-white polka dot fabric remnant

Black embroidery floss

Embroidery needle

Pink thread

WHAT YOU DO

1. Cut eight 5-inch (12.7 cm) squares of pink felt and four 4½-inch (11.4 cm) squares from the fabric.

2. On scrap paper, sketch a heart that's no wider than 4½ inches (11.4 cm) and no taller than 3 inches (7.6 cm). Cut out the heart template.

3. Center the template on a felt square and trace the heart. Remove the template and carefully cut out the heart shape. Repeat for the other felt squares.

4. Pin the fabric squares, right side up, underneath the cut felt so it shows through the heart shape. With the embroidery floss, sew a running stitch around the perimeter of the shapes, ¼ inch (6 mm) from the edge. Turn the coaster over and trim the fabric about ½ inch (1.3 cm) outside the stitches.

5. Pin the coaster back to the front, wrong sides together. Using the pink thread, machine stitch around the perimeter, leaving a ½-inch (1.3 cm) seam allowance. Trim the seams to ¼ inch (6 mm). Repeat with the remaining coasters.

A PENNY (MORE) FOR YOUR THOUGHTS

Although you can use synthetic wool for these coasters, wool felt works best. Spend a little more, and make a gift you'll be proud to give.

pocket placemats

Here are some really cool placemats that have a pocket for silverware. This set of four allows you plenty of room for personalization.

WHAT YOU NEED

Basic Presents Tool Kit (page 11)

1 yard (91.4 cm) of pre-washed fabric

Low-loft batting, 42 x 12 inches (106.7 x 30.5 cm)

¾ yard (68.6 cm) of prewashed accent fabric

Thread that matches both fabrics

Seam gauge (optional)

Skewer or point turner

SEAM ALLOWANCE

¼ inch (6 mm), unless otherwise noted

DESIGNER

LINDSEY M. HAHN

WHAT YOU DO

1 Cut the fabric to size, as follows:

Main fabric: 8 pieces, each 10½ x 12 inches (26.7 x 30.5 cm)

Batting: 4 pieces, each 10½ x 12 inches (26.7 x 30.5 cm)

Accent fabric: 8 pieces, each 6¼ x 3¾ inches (15.9 x 9.5 cm), and 5 pieces, each 2½ x 42 inches (6.4 x 106.7 cm)

2 With two small accent fabric rectangles, fold one short end over ½ inch (1.3 cm) and press. Pin the two right sides together, matching the folded edges. Stitch around the three raw edges using a ½-inch (1.3 cm) seam allowance, backstitching at the beginning and end. Trim the bottom corners and turn the pocket right side out. With the skewer or point turner, poke out the bottom corners neatly. Stitch the top folded edges together, using a ⅛-inch

(3 mm) seam allowance. Repeat to make three more pockets.

3 Mark three lines on one main fabric rectangle: 3 inches (7.6 cm), 6 inches (15.2 cm), and 9 inches (22.9 cm) from a short end. Layer the following: a different main fabric rectangle, right side down; one piece of batting; and the marked main fabric rectangle, right side up. Pin together all three layers, beginning in the middle. Following the lines, quilt stitch through all three layers, removing the pins as you sew. Repeat to make three more placemats.

4 Place the sewn pocket ½ inch (1.3 cm) from the bottom and from the right side of the placemat. Pin it in place. Starting in the upper right corner of the pocket, stitch the pocket to the mat, ⅛ inch (3 mm) from the pocket edge, ending in the

(continued on next page)

upper left corner. Backstitch at the beginning and end. Remove the pins. Repeat to attach the other three pockets.

5 To make double-long bias tape, layer one strip of accent fabric (right side up) and another right side down, creating a right angle. Draw a 45° line from corner to corner. Stitch along the line, backstitching at the beginning and end. Trim off the corner, leaving a seam allowance. Press the seam open, creating a straight piece of bias tape with an angled seam line. Repeat to make three more double-long strips.

6 Fold one bias strip in half lengthwise, wrong sides together, and press. Leaving at least 3 inches (7.6 cm) of a tail, sew the raw edges of the bias strip to the raw edge of the placemat, starting on a long side 2 inches (5.1 cm) from a corner. Pin the strip to the mat if necessary. Stop stitching ¼ inch (6 mm) from the next corner and backstitch. Fold the strip up, creating a 45° angle so that the unsewn strip is pointing away from you, in line with the side of the placemat (figure 1).

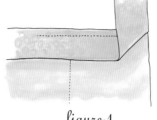

figure 1

7 Fold the strip back down, again lining up the raw edges, and attach it. Continue around the remaining three corners. Stop stitching and back tack less than 2 inches (5.1 cm) after the last corner. To create a nice seam at the end, smooth the two bias tails along the edge of the mat. Mark the point where they meet. Lay them together, right sides facing, and draw a 45° line. Pin the pieces in place and stitch down the line. Trim the corner, leaving a seam allowance. Align the raw edge of the bias tape to the last raw edge of the placemat and sew them together, backstitching at the beginning and end.

8 Fold the bias strip over to the back of the placemat, bringing the folded edge slightly past the stitch line. Pin the strip down and slipstitch the folded edge to the back of the mat. Make the stitches no more than ¼ inch (6 mm) apart. When you reach the first corner, fold it neatly onto itself, and then pin down the next edge before continuing. Work all the way around the placemat. When you return to where you started, knot the thread and trim it close.

9 Repeat steps 6 through 8 to finish the other three placemats.

relaxation therapy

Nothing's more stressful—mentally and physically—than moving into a new place. These hot and cold pads, with their stylish covers, can unwrinkle a brow or soothe an aching muscle.

DESIGNER

CYNTHIA B. WULLER

WHAT YOU NEED

Basic Presents Tool Kit (page 11)

Cotton muslin, ⅛ yard (11.4 cm)

White thread

Sheet of paper, for funnel

Measuring cup

Raw rice, 1½ cups (0.35 l)

2 pieces of cotton quilt fabric in coordinating colors, each ⅛ yard (11.4 cm)

Coordinating thread

WHAT YOU DO

MAKING THE MUSLIN RICE PADS

1 Tear off the selvage edges from the muslin. Measure and mark two pieces, 13 x 4 inches (33 x 10.2 cm), with the grain. Mark the fabric at the edge, snip ½ inch (1.3 cm) on the mark, and then quickly rip the fabric apart.

2 Iron one muslin piece with steam. Fold this piece in half widthwise, matching the corners. Draw a line ½ inch (1.3 cm) from all the raw edges. At the center of the short edge, mark a 2-inch (5.1 cm) opening. Pin or baste along the line, except within the opening. Repeat for the other piece of muslin.

3 Using white thread in the sewing machine and starting from the folded edge of one piece of muslin, straight stitch along the line. Backstitch after the first few stitches to secure the thread. Stop sewing at the opening and backstitch again. Repeat on the opposite side. Repeat on the other piece of muslin.

4 Trim the sewn corners to reduce the bulk, but be careful not to cut the stitching. Turn the pieces inside out. Use the blunt edge of a pencil or the closed end of scissors to push out the corners. Iron the bags flat to remove wrinkles.

5 Make a funnel with the piece of paper. Put the tip into the opening of one bag and fill it with ¾ cup (0.18 L) of rice, which won't completely fill it. Repeat with the other bag.

6 Make sure the folds of the opening are in line with the stitching and then pin or baste the holes closed. Push the rice to the folded edge and machine-stitch the hole closed as close to the edge as possible.

MAKING THE CUSTOM WASHABLE COVERS

7 Cut (or tear as in step 1) two pieces from each piece of quilt fabric, 15½ x 4½ inches (39.4 x 11.4 cm). Iron them all. Fold each piece ½ inch (1.3 cm) in on both short ends, wrong sides together. Press the folds flat. On one end, fold over an additional 1½ inch (3.8 cm) and press it flat.

8 Using a coordinating thread in the sewing machine, zigzag stitch the ½-inch (1.3 cm) folds. Repeat for all pieces.

9 With the wrong side down, turn back the 1½-inch (3.8 cm) flap. Then fold the rest of the piece in half, right sides together, sandwiching the flap in the middle. Line up the edges (figure 1). Pin or baste ½ inch (1.3 cm) in along

figure 1

raw edges only. Straight stitch the seam, making sure to backstitch at the beginning and end of each line. Repeat for all.

10 Turn the covers right side out. Carefully push out the corners. Iron the bags to remove wrinkles.

USING THE RICE PADS

11 To use the rice pads as cold packs, store them in the freezer. To use them as hot pads, microwave the room-temperature pads for about 35 seconds. Always insert the hot or cold pad into a washable cover before using.

12 To insert a rice pad into a cover, fold back the flap and insert the pad. Fold the flap back over the rice pad to keep it in place. Machine wash the covers (but not the rice pads) in cold water on a delicate cycle. Tumble dry low.

REMAINS OF THE DAY

To get all the fabrics you need for this project, check the remnant section of your local fabric store.

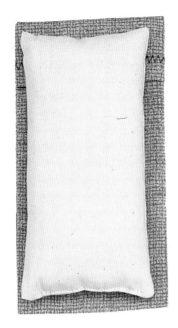

snappy birthday

Smart, spiffy, splendid, stylish—
that's just one letter's worth of
words for these gifts to celebrate
someone's special day.

passport, please

DESIGNER

LISA COX

*T*his is the gift your travel-loving friends never knew they needed until they unwrapped it. It's small enough to fit inside a jacket pocket, but large enough to contain all their important papers.

WHAT YOU NEED

Basic Presents Tool Kit (page 11)

¼ yard (22.9 cm) or one fat quarter each of quilting cotton in two prints (B and C)

Sheet of thin clear plastic (often sold as clear tablecloth plastic)

Medium-weight fusible interfacing

Striped linen (Pattern A), 10½-inch (26.7 cm) square

Solid-colored linen, 4½ x 3¼ inches (11.4 x 8.3 cm)

Thread to match your fabrics

Bias tape maker (optional)

8-inch (20.3 cm) beige zipper

Silver key ring hoop

WHAT YOU DO

1 From the Pattern B quilting cotton, cut out two pieces: one 10½-inch (26.7 cm) square and one 9½ x 10½-inch (24.1 x 26.7 cm) rectangle.

2 From the Pattern C quilting cotton, cut out 13 pieces: five at 1½ x 10½ inches (3.8 x 26.7 cm), one at 1¾ x 2 inches (4.4 x 5.1 cm), two at 2 x 2 inches (5.1 x 5.1 cm), three at 2½ x 22 inches (6.4 x 55.9 cm), one at ½ x 5 inches (1.3 x 12.7 cm), and a last one at 2 x 3 inches (5.1 x 7.6 cm).

3 From the plastic sheet, cut out three pieces: one 4 x 10½ inches (10.2 x 26.7 cm), one 4¾ x 4½ inches (12 x 11.4 cm), and one 4¾ x 5 inches (12 x 12.7 cm).

4 From the interfacing, cut out four pieces: two 10½-inch (26.7 cm) squares, one 9½ x 10½-inch (24.1 x 26.7 cm) rectangle, and one 4½ x 3¼- inch (11.4 x 8.3 cm) rectangle. Iron the interfacing onto the wrong sides of the Pattern A piece, both Pattern B pieces, and the solid linen piece.

5 Press ¼ inch (6 mm) under on all sides of the solid linen. Turn under one short end another ¼ inch (6 mm) and stitch across. Fold the Pattern A fabric in half. With the fold to the left, position the solid linen 1½ inches (3.8 cm) from the bottom and ½ inch (1.3 cm) from the fold. Stitch it down on three sides as shown in the project photo.

PATTERN COMPLEMENTS

While you may choose any complementary fabrics to create your gift, the designer used a brown/ cream linen print (Pattern A), a brown polka dot cotton (Pattern B), and a brown/black floral cotton (Pattern C). Whichever patterns you choose, make sure they all work nicely together.

6 With the 1¾ x 2-inch (4.4 x 5.1 cm) Pattern C piece, form bias tape ⅜ inch (1 cm) wide. Stitch the long open edge closed. Baste the two raw edges together to create a loop. Use the five 1½ x 10½-inch (3.8 x 26.7 cm) Pattern C strips to make more ⅜-inch (1 cm) bias tape, but do not stitch them closed.

7 Center the 2 x 2-inch (5.1 x 5.1 cm) Pattern C pieces over each end of the zipper (near the metal stoppers) with the right side up. Stitch both in place. Fold the fabric over to the back of the zipper tape (figure 1).

8 Wrap a bias strip around the long edge of the large plastic sheet and pin it down. Stitch it ⅛ inch (3 mm) from the inside edge. Pin that edge to one side of the zipper and, using a zipper foot, stitch it ⅛ inch (3 mm) from the edge. Attach a bias strip to the other side of the zipper. Baste the raw edges of the plastic to the left side of the 10½-inch (26.7 cm) Pattern B square, right sides up. Stitch down the zippered side ⅛ inch (3 mm) from the edge, catching the step 6 loop 2½ inches (6.4 cm) from the top.

9 Form a narrow strip of bias tape with the ½ x 5-inch Pattern C piece. Poke it through the end of the zipper and tie a lark's head knot for a zipper pull.

10 Form the 2 x 3-inch (5.1 x 7.6 cm) Pattern C fabric into a bias strip. Stitch the open side closed. Create a loop around the key ring and baste the raw ends along the top edge in the middle of the plastic zippered pocket.

11 Fold the smaller Pattern B fabric in half, wrong sides facing, so it measures 4¾ x 10½ inches (12 x 26.7 cm). Wrap the top short edge of both remaining plastic sheets with a ⅜-inch (1 cm) bias strip. Stitch along both long edges of the bias strip, trimming to fit. Baste the bottom edge of the larger plastic sheet to the bottom edge of the Pattern B fabric with the fold to the left. Wrap a bias strip around the bottom edge of the other plastic sheet and place it on the Pattern B fabric above the other plastic piece. The bound edges of the plastic pieces should align. Fold the bottom piece out of the way and stitch it down along both edges of the bias tape. Stitch a 10½-inch bias strip over the folded edge of the Pattern B fabric with two rows, catching the raw edges of both plastic pockets as you sew (figure 2).

figure 1

figure 2

12 Position the step 11 pouch on the right side of the larger Pattern B fabric and baste it in place along the top, side, and bottom. Layer the whole thing on the Pattern A piece, wrong sides together, and baste them around the perimeter. Join the remaining bias strips and sew them around the outside edges, mitering the corners. Hand sew the inside edge to complete. Do not press the finished wallet.

keep your place

Stitched-in magnets hold this bookmark on its page, but it's your choice of colors and patterns that really does the attracting. Someone in your book group has a birthday coming up? Another present problem is solved.

DESIGNER

JOAN K. MORRIS

WHAT YOU NEED

Basic Presents Tool Kit (page 11)

6 pieces of ½-inch (1.3 cm) wide self-adhesive tape magnet, each 1¼ inch in length

2 pieces of stiff quilt interfacing, each 1¾ x 2⅞ inches (4.4 x 7.3 cm)

Strip of cotton fabric (for the center), 2 x 6 inches (5.1 x 15.2 cm)

2 pieces of cotton fabric (for the background), each 3 x 7 inches (7.6 x 17.8 cm)

Button

WHAT YOU DO

1 Remove the tape backing from one piece of magnet tape and place it ⅜ inch (1 cm) from the short end on a piece of the stiff quilt interfacing. Line up two more magnets below the first, one right next to the other. Repeat on the other piece of quilt interfacing (figure 1).

figure 1

2 Press all the edges of the center fabric piece ½ inch (1.3 cm). Center it on top of one of the background fabric pieces, right sides up, and pin it in place. Machine-stitch all the way around as close as you can to the edge.

3 Place the second background fabric piece on top of the sewn piece, right sides together. Machine-stitch all the way around, ¼ inch (6 mm) in from the edge, leaving a 2-inch (5.1 cm) opening on one of the long sides. Clip the corners.

4 Turn the piece right side out and push out the corners. Press the piece flat, folding under the raw seams. Slide one piece of interfacing through the opening with the magnets facing the back. Push it toward one end of the bookmark. Repeat with the other piece of interfacing, again with the magnets facing the back, but push it toward the other end of the bookmark.

5 Topstitch all the way around, as close as you can get to the edge, catching both sides of the opening. Find the center of the bookmark and topstitch across it. Topstitch ¼ inch (6 mm) in from the first topstitch line, all the way around. Be careful not to catch the magnets. Topstitch across the bookmark ¾ inch (1.9 cm) on either side of the center stitch. Hand stitch the button in place at the very center of the bookmark, where it will fold over.

MAGNETIC ADVICE

When you're sewing with the magnets in the piece, remember that they will be attracted to the metal plate of the sewing machine under the foot. The fabric might stick occasionally while you're sewing, so proceed slowly to get it right.

counting sleep

Give the gift of sleep with this embroidered mask. With simple stitches, you create adorable sheep that tug at the heart and the eyelids.

DESIGNER

BELINDA ANDRESSON

WHAT YOU NEED

Basic Presents Tool Kit (page 11)

Pattern (page 129)

Linen, ⅕ yd (18.3 cm)

Chenille or flannel, ⅕ yd (18.3 cm)

Cotton batting, ⅕ yd (18.3 cm)

Embroidery needle

Embroidery thread, white and black

Strip of cotton, 2 x 16 inches (5.1 x 40.6 cm), for the strap

Safety pin

12-mm elastic, 14 inches (35.6 cm) in length

1-inch (2.5 cm) bias tape, 20 inches (50.8 cm) in length

SEAM ALLOWANCE

¼ inch (6 mm)

WHAT YOU DO

1 Copy the pattern onto the linen, chenille, and cotton batting. Cut one from each fabric.

2 Using a cluster of French knots (page 28) for the bodies and split stitches (page 29) for the legs, embroider sheep onto the right side of the linen.

3 Fold the cotton strap piece in half, right sides together. Stitch the entire length of the strip, backstitching at each end. Turn it right side out using the safety pin. Then press with the seam running down the center; the seam indicates the wrong side of the strap.

4 Insert the elastic into the strap using the safety pin. Zigzag stitch at each end to secure the elastic in place.

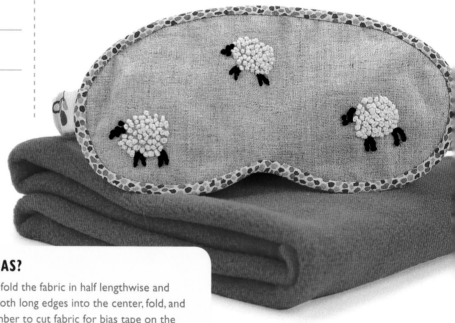

WHAT'S YOUR BIAS?

To make bias tape, fold the fabric in half lengthwise and press. Then bring both long edges into the center, fold, and press again. Remember to cut fabric for bias tape on the diagonal for maximum flexibility.

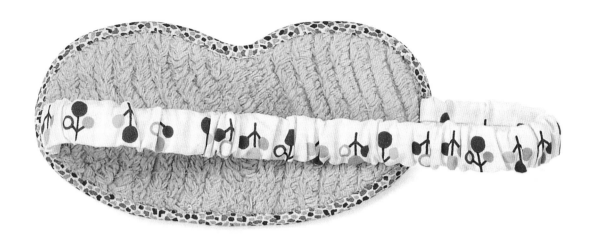

5 Layer the mask pieces as follows (bottom to top): the linen with the right side down, the cotton batting, and the chenille with right side up. Attach the strap to each side of the mask with a zigzag stitch (see the photo above). Ensure the right side of the strap is facing towards you.

6 Starting on the side of the mask, with the linen piece facing you, open the bias tape and fold in the end by ¼ inch (6 mm). Pin the bias tape to the mask, right sides together, using as many pins as you need. When you reach your starting point, overlap the folded end by another ¼ inch (6 mm) and cut off any excess bias tape (figure 1).

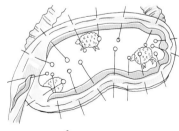

figure 1

7 Stitch the bias tape to the mask. Trim the seam allowance to ⅛ inch (3 mm). Fold the bias tape over and hand-stitch it to the back of the mask.

unforgettable card holder

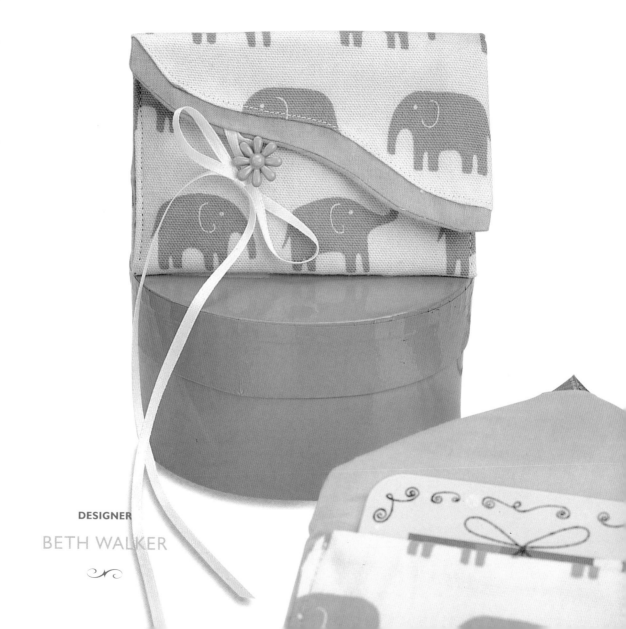

DESIGNER

BETH WALKER

They say elephants never forget, but even Jumbo would have trouble remembering who gave him yet another gift card— if it wasn't in one of these stylish little cases.

WHAT YOU NEED

Basic Presents Tool Kit (page 11)

Pattern (page 129)

2 pieces of complementary fabric, each 10 x 6 inches (25.4 x 15.2 cm)

1 piece of contrasting fabric, 10 x 6 inches (25.4 x 15.2 cm)

Interfacing (optional), 10 x 6 inches (25.4 x 15.2 cm)

Fray retardant (optional)

Ribbon, 20 inches (50.8 cm) in length

Chopstick or knitting needle

A standard gift card, about 3⅜ x 2⅛ inches (8.6 x 5.4 cm)

Button, ¼ to 1 inch (6 mm to 2.5 cm) in diameter

SEAM ALLOWANCE

½ inch (1.3 cm)

WHAT YOU DO

1 Trace and cut out the pattern on scrap paper. Use the pattern to cut the shape from all three fabrics and the interfacing (if you choose to use it). Transfer the pattern marks to the fabric. They show what to leave un-stitched for turning.

2 Put the piece of fabric for the outer shell, right side down, on your ironing board or work space. Fold under the wavy edge ⅛ to ¼ inch (3 to 6 mm). Carefully press the edge down, making sure the wave lies flat and smooth.

3 Lay the contrasting piece of fabric, right side up, on your work space. Add the outer shell fabric on top of it, also right side up. Slide it down so that ¾ inch (1.9 cm) of the contrasting fabric shows. Pin it in place.

4 Stitch close to the folded edge of the outer fabric. Lay the second complementary fabric piece on top of the outer piece so that the wavy edges align. Cut the excess fabric off the other end so that both pieces are now the same size.

POCKET CALCULATOR

Take the time to get the fold just right, so the pocket is large enough to hold the gift card but the overhanging flap lands perfectly when folded.

5 An optional step: Zigzag stitch or use the fray retardant around the edges of both fabric pieces. Iron or stitch the interfacing to the wrong side of the lining fabric (the solid piece, as shown in the photo).

6 Lay the pieces of fabric together with right sides facing. Pin just the sides.

7 Fold the ribbon in half and pinch the center point. Tuck the ribbon between the lining and the outer fabric at the tip of the flap so that only the fold sticks out. The rest of the ribbon should be inside. Pin the ribbon in place.

8 With the ribbons inside away from all seams, sew around the edges, leaving the marked area unstitched. Clip the curves and the corners. Turn the envelope right side out. Use the chopstick or knitting needle to poke the corners out so they are well-defined.

9 Press the fabric to make the edges crisp. Fold the raw seams of the opening in and press them too. Place the piece right side down, with the shaped flap away from you. Fold the bottom edge over about 2½ inches (6.4 cm). Use the business or credit card to ensure that the fold accommodates the card.

10 Fold over the top flap, making sure it looks the way you want it (see the photo at right). When you're satisfied, pin it to the bottom fold. Press both folds and then stitch the sides of the bottom pocket together. Trim the threads and press one more time.

11 Fold the envelope closed and place the button where you think it balances the wavy edge. Sew the button on, making sure it is a little loose so you can wrap the ribbon around it to keep the case closed. Optionally, you can use a little clear glue or fray retardant on the ends of the ribbon.

VARIATIONS

• Instead of using the button, fold the ribbon into thirds and then unfold one end. Attach it the same way to the envelope. Now you can tie it closed, wrapping the longer ribbon around it.

• You can make a simpler version of this card with only two pieces of fabric. Ignore the steps with the contrasting fabric; just create the envelope with an inner lining and an outer shell. As in the variation above, fold the ribbon so you have two-thirds of it to wrap around the envelope to seal it.

• Cut the bottom edge at an angle instead of straight across. Check to be sure it matches the wavy edge so that it completely covers the inside of the envelope.

• Instead of sewing in the ribbon and the button, use adhesive hook-and-eye tape or a snap as a closure. Using a snap, however, means you must reinforce the envelope with the interfacing.

precious cargo

This handmade little carryall shields jewelry (or whatever!) from the rigors of traveling. Make this project as chic or crafty as you wish … it's all in the fabrics and embellishments you choose.

DESIGNER

LISA COX

WHAT YOU NEED

Basic Presents Tool Kit (page 11)

¾ yard (68.6 cm) or 3 fat quarters of quilting cotton in three patterns (A, B, and C)

Lightweight fusible interfacing

Lightweight batting, 8 × 10 inches (20.3 × 25.4 cm)

1-inch-wide (2.5 cm) masking tape

8 inches (20.3 cm) white satin-covered piping

Thread in white and pale blue

Overlocker/serger

2 white zippers, each 7 inches (17.8 cm) in length

8 inches (20.3 cm) thin white rick rack

¾-inch (1.9 cm) white ribbon, 16 inches (40.6 cm) in length

Small drinking glass

¼ to ½-inch (6–13 mm) white ribbon, 30 inches (76.2 cm) in length

¾-inch (1.9 cm) white satin bias tape, 40 inches (101.6 cm) in length

WHAT YOU DO

1 Cut each of the patterned fabrics as follows:

Pattern A: 8 × 10 inches (20.3 × 25.4 cm) and 8 × 8 inches (20.3 × 20.3 cm)

Pattern B: 8 × 10 inches (20.3 × 25.4 cm) and 6½ × 8 inches (16.5 × 20.3 cm)

Pattern C: 5 × 8 inches (12.7 × 20.3 cm), twice

2 Cut the interfacing to match the shapes in step 1. Iron them to the corresponding pieces.

3 Pin the larger Pattern A piece on top of the batting. Machine-quilt them together using a 1-inch (2.5 cm) crosshatch pattern. Set it aside when done.

4 To make the top inside pouch, pin the satin piping to one 8-inch (20.3 cm) edge of the Pattern C fabric, right side up, and baste it in place. Layer the other Pattern C piece on top with the wrong side up and sew it in place. Fold it right side out and press. Overlock, serge, or zigzag stitch across the bottom edge.

5 To make the middle zippered pocket, fold the smaller Pattern B fabric in half, wrong sides together, so it measures 3¼ × 8 inches. With the zipper tab at the left, place the folded edge of the fabric on the zipper tape, below the zipper teeth. Stitch using a zipper foot. Overlock the bottom edge of the pocket. Sew the rickrack 1 inch (2.5 cm) from the bottom edge.

HOLDING PATTERN

While you can choose any complementary fabrics to create your gift, the designer used a blue fabric with red roses (Pattern A), a blue check (Pattern B), and a red polka dot (Pattern C). Patterns work wonderfully with this project; just make sure they all play nicely together.

6 To make the bottom zippered pocket, repeat step 5 using the smaller Pattern A piece and the second zipper.

7 Place the middle zippered pocket (from step 5) on top of the pouch (from step 4), 1 inch (2.5 cm) below the piping. Place an 8-inch (20.3 cm) length of the wider ribbon over the exposed edge of the zipper and sew through all layers along both long edges (see the photo at left).

8 Place the larger Pattern B piece face up. Position the middle zippered pocket/top pouch (from step 7) 1 inch (2.5 cm) below the top. Pin the bottom edge of the pouch to the fabric below it and sew it in place close to the overlocked edge without catching the bottom edge of the pocket (figure 1).

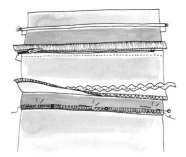

figure 1

9 Place the bottom zippered pouch (from step 6) so the exposed edge of the zipper is sandwiched between the overlocked edge of the top pouch and the overlocked edge of the middle pocket. Layer another 8-inch (20.3 cm) length of the wider ribbon over the overlocked edge of the middle pocket, and sew it in place along both long edges.

10 Trim the bottom edge of the bottom pocket so that the lining piece measures 8 x 10 inches (20.3 x 25.4 cm). Place the entire piece on top of the quilted cover (from step 3), wrong sides together. Baste them together around the edges. Use the drinking glass as a template to draw rounded corners and then trim each corner.

11 Fold the narrower ribbon in half lengthwise, and place the fold in the middle of the top inside edge of the roll and baste it in place. Fold under one end of the bias tape, and then pin it around the outside edge of the jewelry roll. Sew it in place. Fold the bias tape over to the inside edge and hand stitch it in place, making sure to cover the ribbon.

MASKING TAPE TRICK

To help you sew the diagonal crosshatch pattern, place a strip of masking tape at a 45° angle over the fabric as a guide when you machine-quilt. Sew one line at a time, moving the tape as needed.

tying the knot

Let those wedding-shower invitations pour in, now that you have so many great choices for gifts to bring.

initial commitment

DESIGNER

BELINDA ANDRESSON

$\mathcal{H}$ere's a pillow gift that's sure to please. It's like you're carving initials of a special couple into a tree, except no trees are harmed this time around. After all, you're all grown up now (aren't you?).

WHAT YOU NEED

Basic Presents Tool Kit (page 11)

Tracing paper

Transfer pencil

Linen square, 12 x 12 inches (30.5 x 30.5 cm)

Embroidery needle

Red embroidery thread

2 pieces of quilt-weight cotton, 12 x 9½ inches (30.5 x 24.1 cm), for the back

2 strips of matching quilt-weight cotton, 2 x 12 inches (5.1 x 30.5 cm), for the binding

2 fabric-covered shank buttons

Pillow form, 12 x 12 inches (30.5 x 30.5 cm)

SEAM ALLOWANCE

¼ inch (6 mm)

WHAT YOU DO

1 Draw a heart with an arrow through it, and then add the initials of the recipients of this gift. Trace the design onto the tracing paper with the transfer pencil. Pin the design to the front of the linen and iron it on. Using a chain stitch, embroider over the design with the embroidery thread.

2 Fold one of the cotton back pieces ½ inch (1.3 cm) along the longest side from front to back. Press it down. Fold the same side again, 2 inches (5.1 cm) this time. Stitch 1¾ inches (4.4 cm) from the edge. Repeat for the second cotton back piece.

3 On the right side of one back piece, measure 3½ inches (8.9 cm) from each short end and mark the spots with pins (figure 1). Stitch a buttonhole at each mark.

figure 1

4 Lay the back pieces, front side down, with the stitched seam sides overlapping 1 inch (2.5 cm). The buttonholes should be facing out, and the width of both pieces together should measure 12 inches (30.5 cm). Pin the pieces in place.

5 Add the binding around the fabric, mitering each corner (page 23). Start in the middle of one side. Make sure the raw edges of the binding align with the raw edges of the pillow fabric.

6 Mark the placement of the buttons and hand-stitch them in place. Insert the pillow form, wrap it up, and present it to your favorite couple!

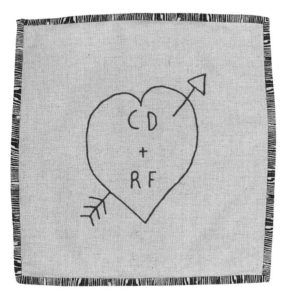

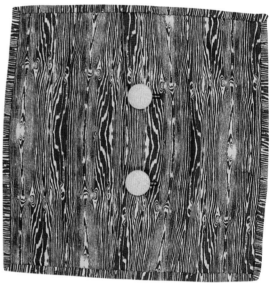

THE PERSONAL TOUCH

Instead of a heart and initials, you can personalize your gift in other ways. For example, you can draw a coffee mug with a message or a T-shirt with a saying. It's not how you draw that matters . . .

wedding memories

Journals to give to bridesmaids, a register for guests to sign, a scrapbook for a honeymoon vacation—a bride-to-be can find so many uses for these classy little albums.

DESIGNER

TERRY TAYLOR

WHAT YOU NEED

Basic Presents Tool Kit (page 11)

Hot pressed or cold pressed watercolor paper

Bone folder or table knife

Phone book

Awl

2 or 3 coordinating fabrics

Waxed linen or heavy thread

2 sharp needles with large eyes

1-inch buttons

WHAT YOU DO

1 Using the ruler, score and tear the watercolor paper into 5½ x 14-inch (14 x 35.6 cm) pieces. You need nine for an 18-page book or 12 for a 24-page book. Stack three or four pieces together, and then fold the stack in half to create a signature that's 5½ x 7 inches (14 x 17.8 cm). Use the bone folder to crease the fold. Make three signatures for each book.

2 Cut a piece of scrap paper into a 5½ x 6-inch (14 x 15.2 cm) rectangle. Fold it in half so it's 5½ x 3 inches (14 x 7.6 cm). Unfold the paper and mark the center point (2¾ inches [7 cm] from the edge) in the crease. Then mark ¼ inch (6 mm) from both edges in the crease. Finally, mark 1¼ inches (3.2 cm) from both edges in the crease.

3 Open the phone book and lay one open signature in the book. Place the scrap paper on top. Use the awl to pierce holes through the signature at the marks. Repeat for each signature. Set the pages aside.

4 Sandwich three layers of fabric, with the top and bottom right sides out. Pin them together.

With the pinking shears, cut a 6 ⅜ x 15¼-inch (16.2 x 38.7 cm) rectangle. Vary each book by using a different fabric on the bottom layer of the stack.

5 Machine-stitch across the width or the length, through all layers, with evenly spaced lines of stitching. Optionally, you may add a second layer of curved lines with a different-colored thread. This is the book cover.

6 Embellish the cover any way you want. For example, stitch strips of coordinating fabric to the cover to create a decorative spine (as shown in the project photo). You can also embroider the cover, sew on appliqués or simple geometric shapes, or any number of other embellishments. The sky's the limit!

7 Create a tie for the book with a 1 ⅛ x 8-inch (2.8 x 20.3 cm) strip of fabric. Fold it in thirds lengthwise and stitch it together with a zigzag or straight stitch. Then machine-stitch the tie to the back cover of the book.

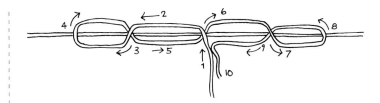

figure 1

8 Fold the book cover in half and iron the folded crease. Slip one signature of watercolor paper into the ironed crease. Cut three 18-inch (45.7 cm) lengths of the waxed linen or heavy thread. Thread a length onto one of the large-eyed needles.

9 Poke the needle through the center hole of the signature, from the inside. Pull the needle through the paper and the cover, leaving a 3-inch (7.6 cm) tail. Back inside the book, poke the second needle without thread into an adjacent hole. Push the tip of the needle through the paper and the cover. Use that tip to show where to stitch the threaded needle back in the cover and through the pages (figure 1).

10 Stitch out through the next adjacent hole and then back down through the previous hole. At the center, stitch up through the hole to the outside. Back inside, poke the unthreaded needle into the adjacent hole on the other side (the side you haven't yet sewn). Pass the threaded needle through the cover and pages at that point. Poke the thread out through the last unstitched hole and back in through the previous hole. Tie the two thread ends together in a small, tight knot.

11 Place another signature page on one side of the stitched stack. Repeat steps 9 and 10 to attach the new signature in place, about ⅛ to ¼ inch (3 to 6 mm) from the first. Repeat with the last signature on the opposite side of the first.

12 Stitch a decorative button in place on the front cover. Wind the tie around the button to seal in the memories.

hearts on a string

ove comes in many forms, but a heart shape speaks clearly, without reservation. You can even skip the final step and give a gift with no strings attached!

DESIGNER

HANNA ANDERSSON

WHAT YOU NEED

Basic Presents Tool Kit (page 11)

2 fabric scraps, any color,
4¼ x 4¾ inches (11 x 12 cm)

Thread in matching color

Stuffing material

Ribbon or household yarn

Big sewing needle (for ribbon or yarn)

WHAT YOU DO

1 Draw or copy a heart-shaped pattern onto scrap paper and cut it out. Make sure the shape fits onto your fabric scraps. Place the paper pattern on the wrong side of one fabric piece and pin it in place.

2 With the pencil, draw around the edges of the pattern onto the fabric. Remove the pattern, but don't cut the fabric yet. Pin the two fabric pieces together, right sides facing. Place the pins within the heart shape.

3 Sew the fabric pieces together, following the pattern line. If you're using a sewing machine, see page 20 for how to turn sharp corners. Leave about ¾ inch (2 cm) open so you can turn your heart right side out.

4 Cut out the fabric heart, about ¼ inch (6 mm) from the seam. Cut small notches into the seam allowance so it will lie flat when it's turned (page 21).

5 Turn the heart shape right side out. Push out all edges using the non-sharp end of the pencil. Stuff it full through the gap with small pieces of the stuffing material. Hand sew along the two edges of the gap to close it, using small stitches.

6 Use the bigger needle to attach the thin ribbon or household yarn at the top of your heart to hang it up.

TAKE THIS TO HEART

This project won't break your bank. Since you need only tiny pieces of any fabric, you don't have to buy anything new. Just recycle your old scraps!

purse your lips

The bride will be the lucky one when she gets this adorable little bag to take along for the honeymoon trip.

DESIGNER

ELIZABETH HARTMAN

WHAT YOU NEED

Basic Presents Tool Kit (page 11)

¼ yard (22.9 cm) of a main printed cotton fabric

⅜ yard (34.3 cm) of a coordinating printed cotton fabric

¼ yard (22.9 cm) of silk

¼ yard (22.9 cm) of lightweight fusible interfacing

Thread in a coordinating color

D-ring, ¾ inch (1.9 cm) in diameter

2 squares of fusible fleece, 11 x 11 inches (27.9 x 27.9 cm)

Elastic hair band

2 buttons, 1 inch (2.5 cm) in diameter

Embroidery floss in a coordinating color

Compass and pencil

2 brooch backs

1 covered button blank, 1½ inches (3.8 cm) in diameter

SEAM ALLOWANCE

½ inch (1.3 cm), unless otherwise noted

WHAT YOU DO

1 Cut the fabric to size, as follows:

Main fabric: 2 pieces, each 6 x 11 inches (15.2 x 27.9 cm), and 2 pieces, each 4 x 11 inches (10.2 x 27.9 cm)

Coordinating fabric: 2 pieces, each 11 inches (27.9 cm) square

Silk and lightweight fusible interfacing: 2 pieces, each 3 x 11 inches (7.6 x 27.9 cm); 2 pieces, each 3 x 4 inches (7.6 x 10.2 cm); 1 piece, 3 x 8½ inches (7.6 x 21.6 cm); and 1 piece, 3 x 15 inches (7.6 x 38.1 cm)

MAKING THE HANDLE

2 Apply the lightweight fusible interfacing to the wrong side of each matching silk piece. Fold the 3 x 15-inch (7.6 x 38.1 cm) piece of silk in half lengthwise, wrong sides together. Open it up, press the raw edges to the middle, and then press it in half again. Repeat with one of the 3 x 4-inch (7.6 x 10.2 cm) silk pieces.

3 Thread the D-ring onto the 15-inch (38.1 cm) handle. Open up both raw ends of the handle and pin them, right sides together. Stitch them together and press the seam open. Refold and press the handle, creating a closed loop. Topstitch close to both edges of the handle.

4 Carefully flatten the loop and wrap the seam ½ inch (1.3 cm) around the flat part of the D-ring. Sew along the seam through all layers of the handle. Stitch it twice.

5 Topstitch both edges of the folded 3 x 4-inch (7.6 x 10.2 cm) silk piece. Thread it through the D-ring and bring the raw ends together. Center the loop on the short side of the other 3 x 4-inch (7.6 x 10.2 cm) silk piece, right

(continued on next page)

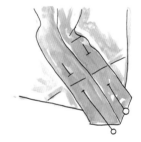

figure 1

side up, and baste it in place. With right sides together and matching 3-inch (7.6 cm) edges, pin the 3 x 8½-inch (7.6 x 21.6 cm) silk strip on top of the handle and stitch through all layers using a ¾-inch (1.9 cm) seam allowance. Press the seam toward the longer piece and topstitch three rows through all layers to secure the handle (figure 1).

MAKING THE PANELS

6 Stitch one 4 x 11-inch (10.2 x 27.9 cm) main fabric piece to the top of the handle panel, right sides together. Stitch one 6 x 11-inch (15.2 x 27.9 cm) main fabric piece to the bottom of the handle panel, arranging the patterns to please. Press the seams open. Fuse one square of fusible fleece to the wrong side of the panel. Topstitch close to the seams between the silk and main fabric on both sides.

7 Lay the finished front panel on a flat surface, with the handle on the left side. Measure and mark 1¼ inches (3.2 cm) in from each top corner. Draw a line from each point to the corresponding lower corner and cut along the lines (figure 2).

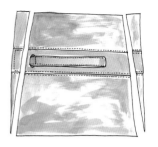

figure 2

8 Stitch the last 6 x 11-inch (15.2 x 27.9 cm) main fabric piece to one of the 3 x 11-inch (7.6 x 27.9 cm) silk pieces, right sides together, along the long side. Then stitch the last 4 x 11-inch (10.2 x 27.9 cm) piece of main fabric, with the pattern upside down, to the other side.

figure 3

9 Fuse the last square of fusible fleece to the wrong side of the back panel. Topstitch close to the seams between the silk and main fabric on both sides. Repeat step 7 with this panel (figure 2 again).

10 Find and mark the top center edge of the back panel. Pinch the sides of the elastic hair band together to create a 2-inch (5.1 cm) loop and a shorter loop. Pin the pinch at the mark so that the smaller loop extends beyond the edge. Sew backward and forward across the elastic several times to secure it. Trim the shorter loop and discard it.

FINISHING THE EXTERIOR

11 On the front panel, center one button 2 ½ inches (6.4 cm) below handle strip. Use the embroidery floss to sew it on securely.

12 Pin the front panel to the back panel, right sides together, and stitch seams along each side and the bottom. Trim the corners and press the seams open.

13 Flatten each bottom corner to a point. Measure 1 inch (2.5 cm) in from that point and draw a line perpendicular to the seam (figure 3). Pin the seams in place and stitch along the line several times. Trim the corners to within ½ inch (1.3 cm) of the sewn line.

MAKING AND ATTACHING THE LINING

14 Lay the two squares of coordinating fabric, right sides together, on a flat surface. Repeat step 7. Using a ⅝-inch (1.6 cm) seam allowance, stitch the sides and bottom together. Repeat step 12.

15 Fold the top edge of the exterior panel over by ½ inch (1.3 cm) and press. Repeat for the lining. Place the exterior and the lining together, matching the bottom seams, and stitch the corners together with a zigzag stitch.

16 Turn the bag right side out. Pin the top edges together, matching the side seams, and topstitch around the top of the bag.

MAKING THE YO-YO EMBELLISHMENTS

17 Use the compass and pencil to draw a 5-inch (12.7 cm) and 6-inch (15.2 cm) circle on the non-fusible side of the lightweight fusible interfacing. Iron the smaller circle on the wrong side of a scrap of silk. Iron the larger circle on the wrong side of a scrap of the coordinating fabric. Trim the circles.

18 Use embroidery floss to hand-stitch a brooch back in the middle of the right side of each circle. Fold over the edges of each circle to the seam allowance and sew a running stitch with regular thread. When you complete the circle, pull the thread to gather the circles into a yo-yo.

19 Starting on one side of the brooch back on the silk yo-yo, sew to the front with embroidery floss that matches the last button, threading it through the button and back to the opposite side of the brooch back. Repeat several times, tie the loose ends together, and trim. Cover the button blank with a scrap of the main fabric.

SHINING THROUGH . . . OR NOT

Back the button blank scrap with a scrap of fusible interfacing to hide the shiny metal.

happy honeymoon

DESIGNER

JOAN K. MORRIS

When your newlywed friends are scanning the luggage carousel at an exotic island airport, spotting their bags will not be a problem.

WHAT YOU NEED

ONLY FOR HIS

Patterns A–D (page 130)

Sandstone felt, 9 x 12 inches (22.9 x 30.5 cm)

Scraps of brown, dark green, and tan felt

1 skein of olive green embroidery floss

ONLY FOR HERS

Patterns E–G (page 130)

Lavender heather felt, 9 x 12 inches (22.9 x 30.5 cm)

Scraps of hot pink, orange, and purple felt

1 skein each of yellow and hot pink embroidery floss

FOR BOTH

Basic Presents Tool Kit (page 11)

2 squares of clear vinyl, 3 inches (7.6 cm) on a side (1 for each tag)

Wax paper

Thread in invisible and off-white

2 large pearl snaps (1 for each tag)

Snap setter

Iron-on double-sided adhesive

Embroidery needle

Thick one-sided interfacing

Press cloth

SEAM ALLOWANCE

¼ inch (6 mm), unless otherwise noted

WHAT YOU DO

1 From one large piece of felt, cut out four pieces: two 3 x 4-inch (7.6 x 10.2 cm) rectangles and two ¾ x 8-inch (1.9 x 20.3 cm) strips.

2 Center a piece of clear vinyl on one of the felt rectangles. Place a slightly larger piece of wax paper on top and sew around three sides of the vinyl, leaving one short side. The wax paper keeps the sewing machine foot from sticking to the vinyl. Pull the wax paper off, making sure to remove any from the stitches. In the center top of the unsewn edge, just above the vinyl, set the male portion of the snap.

SIMILAR BUT DIFFERENT

The instructions are the same for the "His" and "Hers" luggage tags, except for the color of the felt, the color of the embroidery floss, and the drawing of the design.

3 Use the patterns provided or draw your own design. On a piece of scrap paper, outline a rectangle that's 2¾ x 3¾ inches (7 x 9.5 cm). Draw a design to scale, within the rectangle. Cut out the shapes for each color you'll need.

4 With scraps of felt in the appropriate colors that match your design needs, iron on the double-sided adhesive. Use a low temperature setting so you don't melt the felt. Trace your design on the paper backing of the adhesive, remembering to flip the template so you don't reverse the drawings. Cut out each shape.

5 On the other felt rectangle, lay out your design. When satisfied, remove the paper backing and place the pieces adhesive-side-down on the felt. Place one color at a time, background pieces first, ironing them as you go.

6 Zigzag around all the edges with the invisible thread in the top of the sewing machine and the off-white in the bobbin.

Set the zigzag stitch on a medium width and a short length. Catch both the background and the design piece.

7 Embroider onto the design for more detail, as needed. For example, you can embroider the stamen on the flowers with one long stitch for the stem and a French knot at the top.

8 Cut a strip of the double-sided iron-on adhesive that's ¾ x 8 inches (1.9 x 20.3 cm). Adhere it to one of the felt strips. Remove the paper and adhere the other felt strip. Round off one end, cutting through all layers.

9 Lay the felt rectangle with the design face down on a work surface. Place the flat end of the strip on top of it, ½ inch (1.3 cm) down, centered over the top edge. Machine-stitch it in place using invisible thread on the design side. Set the female portion of the snap at the rounded end of the strip, making sure the pearl side is on top (the side with the design).

10 Cut a piece of the double-sided adhesive and the thick interfacing to 3¼ x 2½ inches (8.3 x 6.4 cm) each. Center and iron on the double-sided adhesive to the wrong side of the felt rectangle with the vinyl. Remove the paper backing and place the thick interfacing, adhesive side up. Then place the wrong side of the felt rectangle with the design on the adhesive side of the thick interfacing to make a fabric sandwich.

11 With the press cloth slightly damp, press the sandwich together. Don't worry about the edges. Blanket stitch all the way around the tag with a desired color of embroidery floss. Stitch every raw edge, including the handle. Space the stitches ¼ inch (6 mm) apart.

undercover portfolio

DESIGNER

LISA COX

WHAT YOU NEED

Basic Presents Tool Kit (page 11)

¾ yard (68.6 cm) or 3 fat quarters of quilting cotton in three patterns (A, B, and C)

2 pieces of fusible interfacing, 10 x 18 inches (25.4 x 45.7 cm) and 2½ x 18 inches (6.4 x 45.7 cm)

Satin piping, 18 inches (45.7 cm) in length

Thread in matching colors

Lightweight batting, 12 x18 inches (30.5 x 45.7 cm)

Rickrack, 18 inches (45.7 cm) in length

1-inch-wide (2.5 cm) masking tape

2 zippers, each 12 inches (30.5 cm) in length

2 sheets of clear plastic, each 7½ x 12 inches (19 x 30.5 cm)

⅜-inch (1 cm) satin ribbon, 70 inches (177.8 cm) in length

Small drinking glass

¾-inch (1.9 cm) satin bias tape, 60 inches (152.4 cm) in length

¾-inch (1.9 cm) button

*H*ere's the gift no one has, but everyone will want. Will a bride appreciate this special case for carrying special lingerie on her special honeymoon trip? Oh yes, she will.

WHAT YOU DO

1 Cut each of the patterned fabrics as follows:

Pattern A: 10 x 18 inches (25.4 x 45.7 cm)

Pattern B: two pieces at 2½ x 18 inches (6.4 x 45.7 cm)

Pattern C: 10 x 18 inches (25.4 x 45.7 cm)

2 Iron the interfacing onto the Pattern A piece and one of the Pattern B pieces. Sandwich the piping between the two, right sides together with the corded edge inward. Sew all three together close to the piping with the zipper foot. Press the seams to one side. Set this piece aside.

BEHAVIOR PATTERN

While you can choose any complementary colors to create this present, the designer used an orange, cream, and pink design (Pattern A); a pink and orange spotted pattern (Pattern B); and a pink and cream floral (Pattern C). Choose fabrics you know your recipient will love; just make sure the binding, rickrack, ribbon, thread, and zippers match.

3 Place the second Pattern B piece and the Pattern C piece together, right sides facing, and sew along the long side, using a ¼-inch (6 mm) seam allowance. Press the seams to one side. Layer this piece on top of the batting and pin it in place. Machine-quilt them together using a 1-inch (2.5 cm) crosshatch pattern. Sew the rickrack along the junction of the two fabrics.

4 Overlap one of the zippers with the long edge of one of the plastic sheets and pin in place. Baste them together. Lay a 12-inch (30.5 cm) length of ribbon over the basted edge, and sew one edge over the zipper (with a zipper foot) and the other over the plastic sheet. Repeat for the other zipper and plastic sheet, using another 12-inch (30.5 cm) length of ribbon.

5 Lay both plastic sheets on top of the quilted lining piece, zippers toward the middle so the zippers are about 1 inch (2.5 cm) apart, and pin them all together close to the edges (figure 1). Lay another 12-inch (30.5 cm) length of ribbon over the inside exposed edge of the zipper and sew along both long edges to secure the zipper to the lining. Repeat for the other zipper.

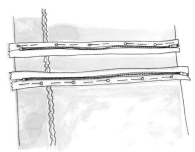

figure 1

MASKING SCHEME

To help you sew the diagonal crosshatch pattern, place a strip of masking tape at a 45° angle over the fabric as a guide when you machine-quilt. Sew one line at a time, moving the tape as needed.

6 Place the lining with zippered pockets on top of the outside cover, wrong sides together. Baste in place around the perimeter, close to the edge. Use the drinking glass as a template to draw rounded corners and then trim each corner, cutting through all layers.

7 With the outside cover face up, place two pieces of 11-inch (27.9 cm) ribbon in the middle of one side edge and baste it in place. Fold one end of the bias tape under ½ inch (1.3 cm), and then wrap it around the entire periphery, pinning it in place as you go. Sew it down through all layers, being careful not to sew through the zipper ends.

8 Sew the button to the opposite edge of the outside cover from the 11-inch (27.9 cm) ribbon. Fold the portfolio in half, and then tie the ribbon around the button to secure it.

bundles of joy

One happy event for new parents—
besides the big one—is sure to be
opening presents as special as these.

gentle waves pillow

DESIGNER

STEPHANIE COSTO

WHAT YOU NEED

Basic Presents Tool Kit (page 11)

½ yard (45.7 cm) of paper-backed fusible web

Blue fabric for the sky,
9 x 13 inches (22.9 x 33 cm)

Patterned fabric for the water,
5 x 13 inches (12.7 x 33 cm)

Patterns (page 129)

Scrap of red fabric for the boat

¼ yard (22.9 cm) of paper-backed fusible web

½ yard (45.7 cm) of large white rickrack

Fabric glue stick for basting

White thread

Scraps of colorful fabric for the sails

5-inch (12.7 cm) piece of fusible fleece

Embroidery hoop

Embroidery needle

Embroidery thread in white and other colors

½ yard (45.7 cm) of fabric for the pillow back

12-inch (30.5 cm) square pillow form

*E*ncourage baby dreams with this whimsical project that's as soft as it is precious. If you've never embroidered before, this pillow is a great place to start.

WHAT YOU DO

1 From the fusible web, cut one piece each to match the sky fabric and the water fabric. Fuse the larger piece to the wrong side of the sky fabric and the smaller piece to the wrong side of the water fabric.

2 Using the sailboat template (A) on page 129, cut one from the red fabric and one from the paper-backed fusible web. Fuse the web to the wrong side of the sailboat fabric.

3 Peel the paper backing from the web and position the sailboat on the sky so that it's 4 inches (10.2 cm) down from the long edge of the sky and ¼ inch from the bottom edge. Fuse the sailboat onto the sky fabric. Machine blanket stitch around the edge of the sailboat with the white thread.

4 Using the ruler and washable fabric pen from your Tool Kit, mark a line ½ inch (1.3 cm) from the bottom edge of the sky. Place the rickrack on top of the line and baste it in place using a long machine stitch or a fabric basting glue stick (figure 1).

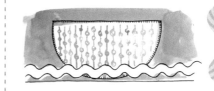

figure 1

5 Place the bottom of the sky along the top (the long side) of the water, right sides together, using a ½-inch seam allowance. Stitch them together, catching the rickrack in the seam. Open the fabric and press the seam toward the water.

6 Fold the boat in half to find its center point. Using a narrow zigzag stitch and white thread, stitch a 3-inch (7.6 cm) pole at the center point.

7 Using the small sail template (B) on page 129, cut out one from the colorful scrap and one from the paper-backed fusible web. Fuse the web to the wrong side of the fabric.

8 Peel the paper backing from the web and position the small sail on the sky to the left of the pole. Fuse the small sail onto the sky fabric. Machine blanket stitch around the edge of the sail with white thread.

9 Using the large sail template (C) on page 129, cut two large sails from the colorful fabric scraps and one from the fusible fleece. Trim the fusible fleece edges by ¼ inch (6 mm) all the way around. Fuse the fleece in the middle of the wrong side of one of the large sails.

10 With right sides together, sew the large sails together using a ¼-inch (6 mm) seam allowance, leaving a 1-inch (2.5 cm) opening at the bottom. Turn the sail right side out by pulling the fabric through the opening. Press the sail, and then topstitch close to the edge all around, closing the opening.

11 Position the large sail on the sky fabric to the right of the pole and pin it in place. Sew only the short vertical side of the sail, stitching over the topstitching.

12 With the washable fabric pen, write the phrase "Sail Away" (or whatever you wish) in the top left corner of the sky. Draw a fish just above the water to the left of the boat. Place the pillow top in the embroidery hoop. Using the embroidery needle and six strands of white embroidery thread, embroider the text. Embroider the fish using another color of embroidery thread.

13 To create the pillow back, cut two pieces of the pillow back fabric, each 11 x 13 inches (27.9 x 33 cm). For each piece, fold the short side over ½ inch (1.3 cm), wrong sides together, and press. Fold the same edge over 1 inch (2.5 cm) and press. Machine stitch the edge using a ¼-inch (6 mm) seam allowance.

14 Overlap one hemmed edge over the other so that the pieces together measure 13 x 13 inches (33 x 33 cm). Baste the sides together.

15 With the right sides together, sew the pillow front to the pillow back with a ½-inch (1.3 cm) seam allowance. Clip the corners and trim the seam, being careful not to clip through the stitching. Turn the pillow right side out and sew the opening closed.

16 Insert the pillow form through the opening in the pillow backing.

SAFETY NOTE

Crib pillows are decorative only. For safety reasons, remove them from the crib whenever the baby is in it.

needlework of art

WHAT YOU NEED

Basic Presents Tool Kit (page 11)

Wooden rod, 48 x ¾ x ⅜ inch
(121.9 x 1.9 x 1 cm)

Heavy-duty stapler

⅓ yard of medium-weight cotton
or linen in white or a light color

Pink and green embroidery thread

Embroidery needle

Patterns (page 130)

5 or 6 scraps of printed fabric

Light pink thread

2 flower buttons

Little button (optional)

Rickrack or ribbon, 6 inches
(15.2 cm) in length

1 medium-sized pink button

String, about 12 inches (30.5 cm)
in length

DESIGNER

CELINE REID

Sewing is an art, so why not frame your work? Try the two designs shown here, or draw and stitch your own original pieces. Your masterpieces will be worthy of hanging in a fine gallery—or nursery.

WHAT YOU DO

1 Cut eight pieces of the rod, each 6 inches (15.2 cm) long. Staple four pieces together as shown in figure 1, keeping the ⅜-inch (1 cm) side on top. Flip the frame over and staple the other side. Repeat to create a second frame.

figure 1

2 Cut two squares from the medium-weight fabric, 10 inches (25.4 cm) on a side. Center a wooden frame on one fabric square, and mark the four corners with a pin to delineate the area for sewing. Repeat for the other fabric square.

3 With tailor's chalk or a water-soluble fabric marker, draw a curved "clothesline" across the sewing area of one fabric square. Using three strands of the pink embroidery thread, backstitch along the line. Then draw two vertical lines, each 1½ inches (3.8 cm) in the bottom left corner. Backstitch over the lines using three strands of the green embroidery thread.

4 Transfer the clothes shapes (patterns A, B, and C on page 130) onto the scraps of fabric and cut them out. Pin them in place just under the clothesline.

Set your sewing machine to make the zigzag stitch narrower and shorter. Then machine-stitch around each piece of clothing. See the project photo for reference.

5 Draw two ¼-inch (6 mm) clothespins on each piece of clothing to attach it to the clothesline. Using three strands of the pink embroidery thread, sew two backstitches for each clothespin. Sew the flower buttons on top of the stems, and if you want to add a little button to decorate the shirt, do so now.

6 On the second fabric square, sew the rickrack in the bottom left, using a straight stitch all the way to the edge.

7 Transfer the flower and butterfly shapes (patterns D, E, and F on page 130) onto more scraps of fabric and cut them out. Pin the flower on top of the rickrack and the butterfly wings to the right of the flower.

8 Repeat step 5, stitching a zigzag around each shape. Stitch around the butterfly wings first, and then pin the body on top and stitch it in place. Sew the medium-sized button in the middle of the flower.

9 draw two antennae at the top end of the body. With three strands of the green embroidery thread, backstitch over the lines. Add a French knot at the tip of each antenna.

10 If you haven't marked it before, draw the butterfly's line of flight. With three strands of the pink embroidery thread, stitch along the line using a running stitch.

114

11 Secure one fabric square on a wooden frame by stapling the fabric to the back of the frame, starting in the middle of each opposite side, working your way towards the corners. Cut the string in two and then tie a knot at each end. Staple the string on each side of the frame, about a third of the way from the top (figure 2).

figure 2

PRACTICE MAKES PERFECT

Because each sewing machine is different, check your manual for adjusting stitches. Also, before you stitch on your pretty little present, try the setting out on a spare piece of fabric. Practice until you're happy with the results.

nesting instinct

$\mathcal{T}$his Mom and Baby pair of birds is sure to stay together, while the useful tote keeps together all the little things needed for an afternoon out.

DESIGNER

MARINA ROUSSEL

WHAT YOU NEED

Basic Presents Tool Kit (page 11)

Patterns (page 127)

2 remnants of cotton fabrics with complementary patterns

½ yard (45.7 cm) of natural-colored linen

3 different ribbons that complement the cotton remnants: 5½ inches (14 cm), 11 inches (27.9 cm), and 18 inches (45.7 cm)

Chopstick or knitting needle for shaping

Cotton, wool, or polyester stuffing

Thread in a neutral color

2 strips of natural-colored crochet lace trim, 10 inches (25.4 cm) and 9 inches (22.9 cm)

1-inch (2.5 cm) self-covering button

Thread that matches or complements the linen

Two rectangles of calico- or cream-colored cotton, 10 x 9 inches (25.4 x 22.9 cm)

SEAM ALLOWANCES

¼ inch (6 mm) for the birds

½ inch (1.3 cm) for the tote

WHAT YOU DO

MAKING THE BIRDS

1 Using the mother bird template (A), cut the shape from one of the cotton remnants and one from the linen. Repeat, using the baby bird template (B) and cutting from the other cotton remnant and the linen.

2 Using the fabric marker, make two small lines near the raw edge on the right sides of both linen shapes to indicate where to place the ribbon tags, as shown on the template. Repeat on the wrong sides of both cotton shapes to indicate where to leave the openings for turning and stuffing, also as shown on the template.

3 Cut the 11-inch (27.9 cm) ribbon in half and fold each in half to make a loop. Place the mother bird linen right side up. Center the ribbon loops over the marks and pin them to the linen, centered over the marks with the raw edges aligned, so the looped ends lie inside the bird body (figure 1).

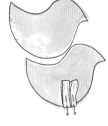

figure 1

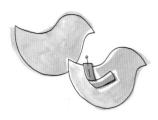

figure 2

4 Repeat step 3 with the 5½-inch (14 cm) ribbon and the baby bird linen. Fold the ribbon at an angle in the center of the shape and pin it down from the back of the fabric (figure 2) so you don't sew over the ribbon as you stitch around the shape's edge.

5 Place the patterned cotton pieces, right side down, on top of the matching linen pieces. Pin them in place. Carefully sew the pieces together, leaving the openings indicated. Backstitch a few times as you start and finish the seams. Trim the excess fabric from the pointy tip of the beaks and tails within the seam allowance without cutting the stitching.

6 Turn the pieces right side out, using the chopstick or knitting needle to gently poke the fabric into shape. Turn under the raw edges and press both shapes flat. Starting with the head, fill each bird with stuffing, a small amount at a time. When the birds are plump, hand-stitch the openings closed using the neutral-colored thread.

7 Turn over each raw edge of the 10-inch (25.4 cm) strip of crochet lace trim and press. Place one end of the trim on the linen at the neck and make a few stitches to hold it in place. Pull the other end around the neck and overlap it. Stitch this collar along the length of the trim.

8 Cover the button with a matching fabric scrap and assemble it. Sew the button to the top front of the baby bird's ribbon loop.

MAKING THE TOTE

9 Cut two rectangles from the linen, 10 x 9 inches (25.4 x 22.9 cm). Cut two linen strips, 12 x 2½ inches (30.5 x 6.4 cm). Cut the remaining ribbon in half.

10 Starting 2 inches (5.1 cm) down from one raw edge, pin both ribbons and the 9-inch (22.9 cm) crochet lace trim onto the right side of one of the linen rectangles, one underneath the other. Sew along the edges of each strip with matching or complementary color thread.

11 Pin the linen rectangles together, right sides facing, and sew around the sides and bottom. Trim the bottom corners within the seam allowance. Press the seams open and then turn the tote right side out, gently pushing out the bottom corners.

12 Repeat step 11 to make the lining out of the cotton rectangles, but leave a 3-inch (7.6 cm) opening in the bottom seam for turning. Press the seams open. Leave the lining wrong side out.

13 Fold the handle strips in half lengthwise and press them to make a crease. Open and press them again lightly. Turn each long edge over ¼ inch (6 mm) and press. Re-fold each strip at the crease line, press, and pin. Topstitch along each long edge.

14 Pin the finished handles to the front and back of the linen bag, 1 inch (2.5 cm) in from the side, aligning the raw edges. Sew across the end of each handle ¼ inch (6 mm) in from the edge.

15 Place the linen bag inside the cotton bag, with the handles tucked neatly down in between the two layers. Line up the side seams and pin the top raw edges together. Sew around the top edge of the bag.

16 Turn the bag through the opening in the bottom of the lining, and then sew the opening closed. Tuck the lining into the tote and press. To finish, topstitch around the top of the tote, especially under the handles. Tie the baby bird onto one of the handles with the last piece of ribbon.

wake, rattle & stroll

DESIGNER

ROXANNE BEAUVAIS

*P*laced around the wrist or clutched in a chubby little hand, this flowery rattle gives a new mom the greatest gift of all: a quiet and happy baby.

WHAT YOU NEED

Basic Presents Tool Kit (page 11)

Petal pattern (page 130)

3 coordinating or contrasting cotton fabrics, each 6 x 8 inches (15.2 x 20.3 cm)

White thread

Polyester fiberfill

24 jingle bells, each ⅜ inch (1 cm)

Safety Pin

⅜-inch (1 cm) wide elastic, 8 inches (20.3 cm) in length

HIDE AND SEEK

To keep the elastic hidden even when stretched, hand stitch the petals together with matching thread. A couple of quick stitches on both sides of each petal will do the trick.

WHAT YOU DO

1 Cut out four pattern pieces in each fabric, totaling twelve petals.

2 Pin two matching petals, right sides together. Mark 1 inch (2.5 cm) down on either side of the petal. Sew around the petal from marked spot to marked spot with a ½-inch (1.3 cm) seam allowance. Keep the needle down when you shift the fabric around the curve.

3 Notch the seam allowance around the curve, and then turn the petal right side out. Press it flat. Tuck the raw edges in as you iron so the sides are even all the way up. Fold the straight edges down ¼ inch (6 mm) on the short end and press.

4 Stuff fiberfill and four jingle bells into the petal up to the marked 1-inch (2.5 cm) point. Pin the petal at the marked point and topstitch across. Sew another seam as close to the top straight edge as possible, creating a casing.

5 Repeat steps 2 to 4 to create five more petals, making sure to use different fabrics.

6 Arrange the petals in an alternating fabric pattern. Attach the safety pin to the end of the elastic and thread it through the casing of each petal in turn. Pull the elastic tight to create a gathered effect (see the photo at left).

7 Pin and sew the ends of the elastic together several times. Distribute the petals evenly around the elastic.

time *for a change*

New parents won't be truly delighted
every time they need to pull out this pouch for
diapers and their accessories (you know why),
but they will appreciate its sharp looks
and convenient design.

DESIGNER

LINDSEY M. HAHN

WHAT YOU NEED

Basic Presents Tool Kit (page 11)

¼ yard (22.9 cm) or 1 fat quarter of prewashed coordinating fabric

Prewashed main fabric, 21¾ x 8 inches (55.2 x 20.3 cm)

Thread that matches the main fabric

Bottle of spray starch (optional)

Skewer or point turner

SEAM ALLOWANCE

¼ inch (6 mm)

WHAT YOU DO

1 Cut the coordinating fabric to size as follows: one lining at 21¾ x 8 inches (55.2 x 20.3 cm); one bias strip at 21¾ x 2½ inches (55.2 x 6.4 cm); and two bias strips at 21¾ x 2 inches (55.2 x 5.1 cm).

2 Pin the main fabric piece to the lining piece, wrong sides together, matching the raw edges. Fold the wider bias strip in half widthwise, wrong sides together, and press.

3 Line up the raw edges of the bias strip with those of the short (top) side of the main fabric and lining. Pin all four layers and stitch together, backstitching at the beginning and end. Trim the bias strip (figure 1).

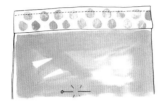

figure 1

4 Remove the pins and press the bias over the stitching. If desired, use the spray starch. Press the folded edge of the binding to the back, making sure it extends beyond the stitching line. Use the spray starch again and press the bias firmly in place.

5 Stitch the main fabric right up against the bias strip, catching the bias in the back. Make sure you catch the bias strip edge in the back completely. Backstitch at the beginning and end.

6 With the remaining piece of the bias strip, repeat steps 3 to 5 with the opposite short end of the main fabric/lining piece.

7 Leaving the pins in the main fabric/lining, lay it main fabric side up on your work space. Fold the top down 3½ inches (8.9 cm) and the bottom up 7¾ inches (19.7 cm). The bound short ends should overlap slightly. Line up the raw edges on both sides and pin them in place. Stitch them together, backstitching at the beginning, at the end, and over the bias strips.

8 Fold both of the remaining bias strips in half widthwise, wrong sides together, and press. Open one raw end, tuck in ¼ inch (6 mm), and press it in half again. Trim each strip to 10½ inches (26.7 cm) long, and then press the other raw edge in ¼ inch (6 mm). Pin one bias strip to a long raw edge of the pouch. Stitch through all layers.

9 Repeat steps 4 and 5 for this edge. Then add the last piece of bias tape to the final raw edge in the same way.

10 Turn the pouch right side out and remove the rest of the pins. Use the skewer or point turner to push out the corners neatly. Press the entire pouch flat.

hello, doll faces

*I*nspired by those sets of Russian dolls that fit inside one another, this string of uniquely smiling faces will delight and reassure any baby out for a stroll.

DESIGNER

BELINDA ANDRESSON

WHAT YOU NEED

Basic Presents Tool Kit (page 11)

Doll patterns (page 130)

Scraps of quilt-weight cotton totaling ⅕ yd (18.3 cm), for the doll bodies

Cream-colored wool felt, 5 inches (12.7 cm) square, for the doll faces

⅜-inch (9.5 mm) satin ribbon, 38 inches (96.5 cm) in length

Matching machine thread

Embroidery needle

Embroidery thread, red and brown

Chopstick

Polyfill

1½-inch (3.8 mm) satin ribbon, 56 inches (142.2 cm) in length

2 large safety pins

½-inch (1.3 mm) elastic, 25 inches (63.5 cm) in length

2 silver bells

SEAM ALLOWANCE

¼ inch (6 mm)

WHAT YOU DO

1 Cut eight body patterns from the cotton and four face patterns (both, page 130) from the wool felt. Cut four 2-inch (5.1 cm) pieces from the narrow ribbon.

2 Sew the wool felt faces in place to the right side of four bodies. Use straight, zigzag, or blanket stitches. Embroider the hair and facial features as shown in the project photograph.

3 Lay one ribbon right side down on top of one doll front, with the top of the ribbon flush with the top raw edge. Then layer one doll back (right side down) on top, sandwiching the ribbon between the front and back. Sew the pieces together, leaving a 1-inch (2.5 cm) opening.

4 Clip the corners and iron back the seam allowance at the opening.

5 Turn the doll right side out. It won't be easy with such a small opening. Tease out as much fabric as you can, and then use the ribbon to pull out the rest of the body. Using the chopstick, make sure all the curves and corners are fully turned out. Then stuff the doll body with the polyfill and sew the opening closed. Trim the ribbon to 1¼ inches (3.2 cm).

6 Repeat steps 3 to 5 to create three more stuffed dolls.

7 Next, fold the wide ribbon in half with the wrong sides together, and then press. Pin each doll along the wide ribbon at the following intervals: 5 inches (12.7 cm) from one end, 6 inches (15.2 cm) from that point, 6 more inches (15.2 cm), and finally 6 inches (15.2 cm) after that. There should be 5 inches (12.7 cm) remaining.

MIX AND MATCH

You don't have to use the same color fabric for the front and back of each doll's body. In fact, it's better if you don't. Try different fabric patterns and colors together to find pleasing combinations. These dolls are folk art incarnate.

8 Add pins between dolls and sew the ribbon closed using a ⅛-inch (3 mm) seam allowance to secure the dolls and form a casing for the elastic.

9 Using the safety pin and thread, insert the elastic into the casing. When you have pulled the full length of the elastic through, secure each end with a safety pin.

10 Turn in one end ¼ inch (6 mm) and insert a 9-inch (22.9 cm) length of the narrow ribbon inside, in front of the elastic (figure 1). Secure it with a zigzag stitch across the opening. Make sure you catch the turned-in edge, the elastic, and the ribbon ties. Repeat on the other end.

figure 1

11 Distribute the wide ribbon so it's evenly gathered across the casing.

12 Use the remaining narrow ribbon to fashion bows on each end of the casing to cover the zigzag stitching. Secure them with a couple stitches. To finish, stitch one of the bells securely to each end.

templates

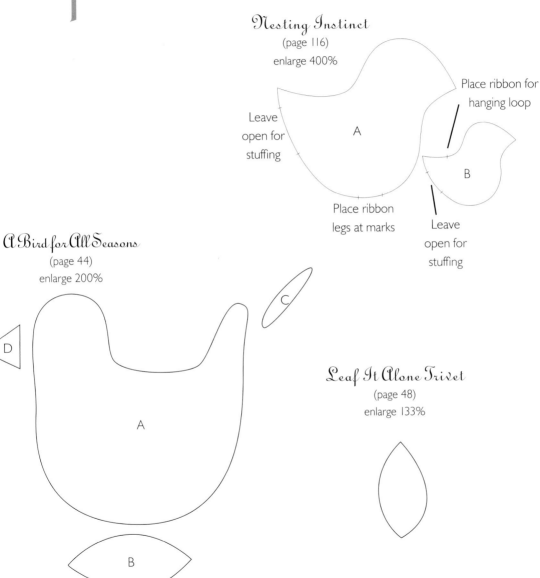

Nesting Instinct
(page 116)
enlarge 400%

A

Leave open for stuffing

Place ribbon for hanging loop

B

Place ribbon legs at marks

Leave open for stuffing

A Bird for All Seasons
(page 44)
enlarge 200%

C

D

A

B

Leaf It Alone Trivet
(page 48)
enlarge 133%

Sew Convenient

(page 35)

enlarge 300%

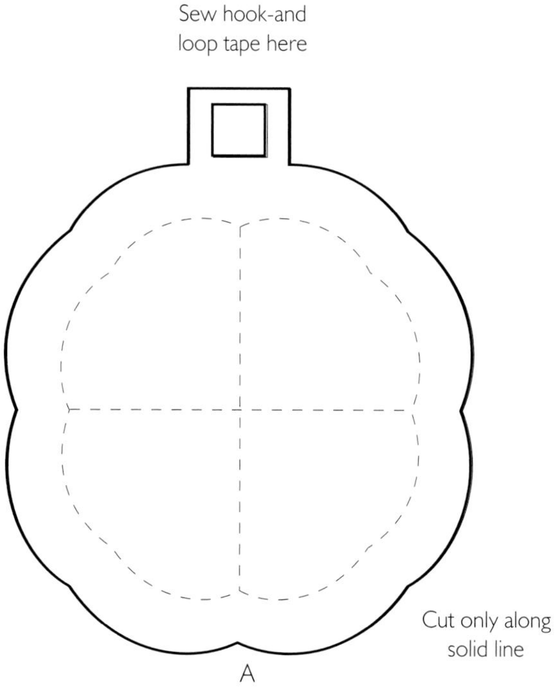

Sew hook-and
loop tape here

Sew along these lines

Cut only along
solid line

A

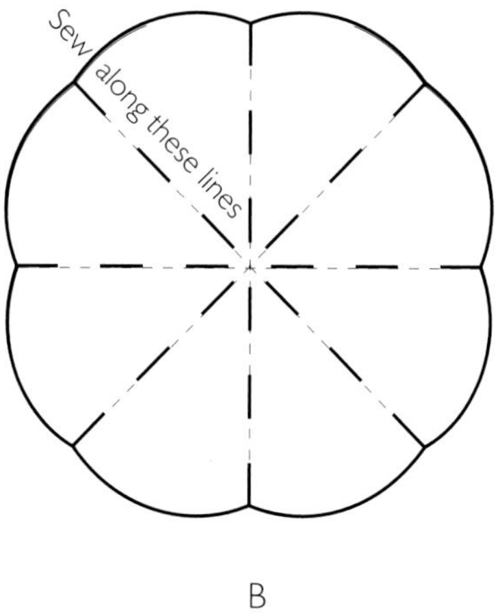

B

All Buttoned Up

(page 42)

enlarge 133%

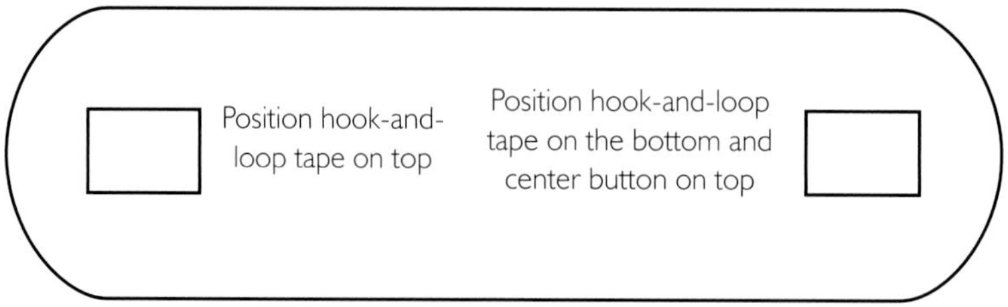

Position hook-and-
loop tape on top

Position hook-and-loop
tape on the bottom and
center button on top

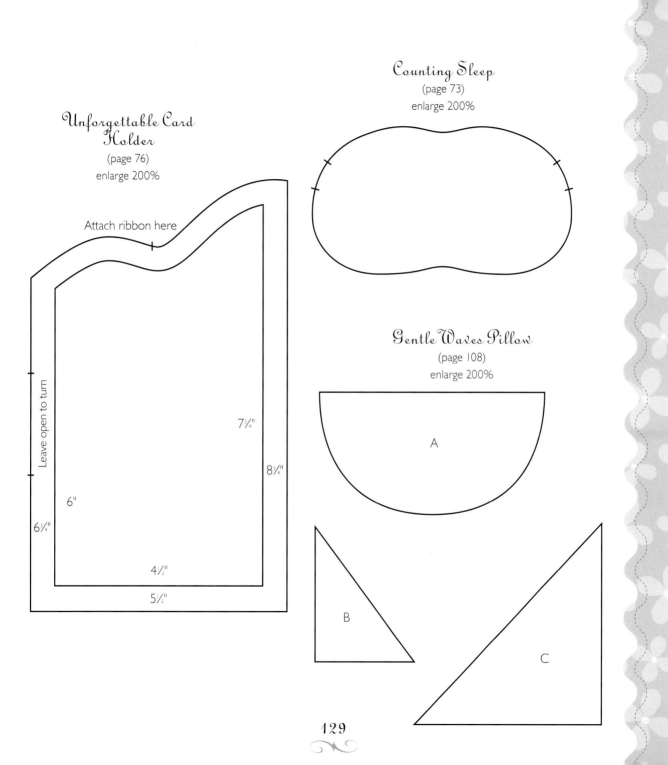

Unforgettable Card Holder
(page 76)
enlarge 200%

Attach ribbon here

Leave open to turn

7¾"

8¾"

6"

6¾"

4½"

5½"

Counting Sleep
(page 73)
enlarge 200%

Gentle Waves Pillow
(page 108)
enlarge 200%

A

B

C

Needlework of Art
(page 112)
enlarge 200%

A B C

D E F

Hello, Doll Faces
(page 124)
enlarge 200%

A

B

Happy Honeymoon
(page 98)
enlarge 200%

Middle circles
are holes

E
F

G H

C

D

A

B

Wake, Rattle & Stroll
(page 120)
enlarge 400%

1" 1"

aboutthedesigners

KATHERINE ACCETTURA designs purses, pouches, and baby items. She sells her wares on www.kateyez.etsy.com and blogs at www.craftfriendlyso-il.blogspot.com.

HANNA ANDERSSON runs a web shop with her mother called I Shop with Mom (www.ihanna.nu) where they sell their art and hand-made products.

BELINDA ANDRESSON writes about her craft projects at www.tuttifruiti.blogspot.com and at tuttifruitidesigns.wordpress.com.

WENDY ARACICH runs an online boutique, Circle Circle Dot Dot (www.circlecircledotdot.com).

ROXANNE BEAUVAIS has an online shop of vintage fabric and unique designs at www.feminineaddictions.etsy.com and a blog at www.craftaddictions.blogspot.com.

STEPHANIE COSTO shows her latest creations at www.stephanielynnstudio.blogspot.com. She also sells her things at www.creativereveries.etsy.com.

LISA COX has been an avid crafter since childhood. She and her daughter Sarah collaborate on the blog www.spoonfullofsugargirls.blogspot.com, where you can follow their adventures.

LINDSEY M. HAHN has a BA in fashion design, but her real passion is crafting. You can find her daily at www.linques.typepad.com, and visit her online shop at www.lindseymarcella.etsy.com.

ELIZABETH HARTMAN is a self-taught sewer, pattern designer, and crafter. See her craft blog, www.ohfransson.com, for her quilts, bags, and household items. Visit her shop at www.ohfransson.etsy.com.

FIONA HESFORD has a passion for all things funky and colorful. Her work has been featured in the Elle Decoration and Marie Claire U.K. magazines. See her website at www.girls-institute.co.uk.

JOAN K. MORRIS has contributed projects for many Lark Books books, like *Cutting-Edge Decoupage, Pretty Little Pincushions, Button! Button!, Pretty Little Potholders,* and *50 Nifty Beaded Cards.*

CELINE REID is a self-taught artist. She loves using recycled material whenever she can. Read her thoughts at her blog (applejuice.canalblog.com) and visit her store at www.applejuicegifts.co.uk.

MARINA ROUSSEL designs a line of children's gifts and housewares under the label Wink Designs (www.winkdesigns.com.au). Marina also keeps an online journal at www.winkdesigns.typepad.com.

TERRY TAYLOR is an acquisitions editor at Lark Books. He's also the author of several books, including *Altered Art, Artful Paper Dolls, The Altered Object,* and *Button! Button!* (all by Lark Books).

CANDACE TODD fills her days with mothering, sewing, cooking, and searching for vintage treasures. She posts all about it on her blog, which she invites everyone to visit, at candacetodd.blogspot.com.

BETH WALKER sews, embroiders, and knits quirky accessories. Some of them are in shops under the label Ask a Marmot Designs. Beth is a member of the TACTILE Textile Arts Center in Denver.

CYNTHIA B. WULLER'S work has appeared in *The Art of Jewelry: Paper Jewelry, The Art of Jewelry: Wood, Beading with Pearls,* and *Stitched Jewels,* all by Lark Books. She is also the author of *Inspired Wire.*

acknowledgments

It took many people to make this book look as good as it does. Thanks, first of all, to the talented designers who contributed their imaginative and beautiful pretty little projects to this book. A big round of applause for sharing your brilliant talents and inspiring us all!

Thanks also to Lark Books' dedicated editorial team: Larry Shea, Gavin Young, Mark Bloom, and Jessica Boing. Megan Kirby's art direction provided a beautiful setting for the book's words and images, and Jeff Hamilton's art production made it all come true. A final thanks to those who helped make the book as lovely as it could be: Susan McBride for her sweet little illustrations, Orrin Lundgren for his masterful templates, Stewart O'Shields for his perfect photography, and Megan Cox for not only assisting Stewart but modeling with such panache! Rebekah Cecile MacNair also delivered her talents as a model and deserves our thanks.

index

It's all on www.larkbooks.com

Can't find the materials you need to create a project? Search our database for craft suppliers & sources for hard-to-find materials.

Got an idea for a book? Read our book proposal guidelines and contact us.

Want to show off your work? Browse current calls for entries.

Want to know what new and exciting books we're working on? Sign up for our free e-newsletter.

Feeling crafty? Find free, downloadable project directions on the site.

Interested in learning more about the authors, designers & editors who create Lark books?